ENGLISH
ROMANESQUE
ARCHITECTURE

DURHAM CATHEDRAL, N. SIDE OF NAVE

ENGLISH ROMANESQUE ARCHITECTURE

AFTER THE CONQUEST

By A. W. CLAPHAM, F.S.A.

OXFORD
AT THE CLARENDON PRESS

Oxford University Press, Ely House, London W.1

GLASGOW NEW YORK TORONTO MELBOURNE WELLINGTON
CAPE TOWN SALISBURY IBADAN NAIROBI LUSAKA ADDIS ABABA
BOMBAY CALCUTTA MADRAS KARACHI LAHORE DACCA
KUALA LUMPUR SINGAPORE HONG KONG TOKYO

FIRST PUBLISHED 1934
REPRINTED LITHOGRAPHICALLY AT THE UNIVERSITY PRESS, OXFORD
FROM SHEETS OF THE FIRST EDITION
1964, 1969

PRINTED IN GREAT BRITAIN

PREFACE

BUT few words are needed as a preface to this volume, which is indeed only a continuation of a previous one dealing with English Romanesque Architecture before the Conquest. The method of approach to the subject will, however, be found somewhat different as indeed the case demands. The previous period is sparsely documented and its surviving buildings comparatively few and scattered; on the other hand its affinities are broad and almost European in their extent. The post-Conquest period, on the contrary, is fairly fully documented and its examples are numerous. Its affinities, however, are restricted, and architecturally at least it forms the full development of the Norman school largely untouched by other influences before the middle of the twelfth century. Its background therefore lacks the many-toned variety of that of the earlier age and its study becomes of necessity more purely architectural.

The foundations of the study of our native medieval architecture were well and truly laid by Professor Willis in the forties of the last century, and it is a remarkable tribute to his perspicacity and common sense that modern criticism has hardly ever an opportunity of doing other than approve his conclusions. Unfortunately his published studies cover only a few of our great buildings, and many of those which he left unconsidered have remained to the present day without an adequate and scientific survey. The study so well begun by Professor Willis has been continued by a number of distinguished antiquaries, of whom we may notice the late Sir W. St. John Hope and Mr. Mickelthwaite and, among those living, Dr. John Bilson, Sir Harold Brakspear, and Sir Charles Peers.

It may be urged, and to some extent rightly urged, against the presentation of the subject in the following pages, that not enough prominence has been given to the purely structural aspects of Anglo-Norman architecture. In reply to this I can only urge that the book is not primarily intended for architects, and that the technicalities of building-construction, constructive equilibrium, and other matters of a like nature, necessitate too intricate and involved a description to be suited to a general work. For this reason I have abstained from reproducing architectural sections or diagrammatic drawings; such illustrations, though clear enough to the professional eye, are less apt to be intelligible to the general reader and are perhaps more appropriate to monographs on individual buildings or purely technical treatises. The plans, in conjunction with the photographic illustrations, should be sufficient to explain the general form and structure of the buildings under review, more especially as but one great Romanesque church in the country retains any great part of its original high vaulting.

It is perhaps necessary to explain that this book is concerned with Ecclesiastical architecture and touches only on secular buildings of the same age when they throw some light on the evolution of mouldings and detail.

The plans in the book are reproduced to a uniform scale of 48 feet to the inch, the surviving or recovered portions of the building being shown in solid black. In general, the Gothic and later modifications and additions have been omitted.

In the preparation of this book I am deeply indebted to a number of people who in one way or another have added greatly to its accuracy. First among these is Dr. John Bilson, whose lifelong study of the subject has rendered him the only fit and proper person to have written such a work. I gratefully acknowledge his constant and ungrudging assistance, and if I have not at all times agreed with his conclusions it is not that I do not admit that they should carry greater weight than my own. To my other friends Sir Charles Peers, Dr. Rose Graham, and Mr. J. McNeil

Rushforth, I am indebted for reading in whole or in part the proofs of this volume and for many valuable additions and corrections.

In regard to the illustrations I have to acknowledge the kindness of Mr. W. H. Knowles, F.S.A., in allowing me the use of his plan of Kempley Church, Mr. J. S. Richardson for his drawing of the pavement in Byland Abbey, and of Dr. Fairweather for his plans of Binham, Hales, &c. Also of Mr. Arthur Gardner, Mr. R. Griffin, Mr. G. E. Chambers, Mr. J. R. H. Weaver, and Mr. P. K. Kipps in permitting me to use their photographs. The plans of Tintern, Rievaulx, Byland, Lindisfarne, and Roche are based on those of the Ancient Monuments Department of H.M. Office of Works, through the kindness of the then Chief Inspector, Sir Charles Peers.

As in the previous volume I am deeply indebted to Miss V. M. Dallas for compiling the index.

A. W. C.

February 1934

CONTENTS

LIST OF FIGURES IN THE TEXT

LIST OF PLATES

Chapter I

THE BEGINNINGS OF NORMAN
ROMANESQUE

REVOLUTIONARY as was the effect of the Norman Conquest on the civil and political status of the English it was even greater and more far-reaching in the realms of art and learning. The new Norman hierarchy, which, with few exceptions, dispossessed the native ecclesiastics within a few years of the Conquest brought with it an established order both of church-governance and architecture which, almost without effort, overthrew the loosely-knit organization and somewhat haphazard architecture of the Anglo-Saxon Church. The semi-religious character with which the policy of the Conqueror succeeded in investing his expedition involved the Saxon Church in the ecclesiastical censure of the unfortunate Harold and contributed to render the Norman Conquest as complete intellectually as it was politically. Hardly ever before or since has a national culture been so easily, so rapidly, or so completely submerged as was the Anglo-Saxon in the last thirty years of the eleventh century. Here and there the old traditions lingered on but by the time the last entry of the Saxon Chronicle was penned the last trace of Saxon art or architecture had disappeared. The completeness of the change is evidence not only of a lack of vitality in the native art but a convincing testimony to the strength and cohesion of its supplanter; the Saxon spirit was an uncreative one, which required from time to time an infusion of fresh ideas to galvanize it into activity. This, as we have seen, was provided successively by the Eastern influences of the seventh century; by the Carolingian revival and by the strong barbaric admixture of Scandinavian art. Of these, the first was planted in virgin soil, but the other two guided and re-vivified rather than supplanted the native growth. The Norman art, on the other hand, backed by both the temporal and spiritual power swept everything before it and produced a homogeneous and nearly universal culture in which one encounters only here and there the vague ghosts of earlier things clothed in a new garb and only recognizable from their unfamiliarity in the native art of Normandy.

There had been some slight infiltration of Norman architectural ideas before the Conquest actuated by the proximity of the two countries and furthered by the Normanizing tendencies of Edward the Confessor. This king did his best to install his favourite foreigners in English dioceses and a few of these such as William of London and the Lorrainers[1] in the west country maintained their place until after the Conquest; it was, however, in the building of the abbey-church of Westminster that the Confessor contributed directly to the introduction of the foreign style. The church at Westminster was so far as we know a close copy of the churches of half a dozen Benedictine abbeys of Normandy of nearly the same age and it is possible that the example of the king found imitators amongst the native nobility. We know that at the same time Harold was building a minster at Waltham and Leofric another at Coventry, but unfortunately all remains of these have disappeared.

The art which the Norman conquerors introduced was mainly the pure product of Normandy; but just as Duke William's army included recruits from various provinces so the earliest architecture of the invaders, though essentially and predominantly Norman, shows signs of more varied sources.

The church-architecture which was the result of the Carolingian religious and artistic revival, was a conscious

---

[1] Hermann of Sarum, Gisa of Wells, Walter of Hereford, and (by education) Leofric of Exeter.

renaissance of earlier and Roman forms. The great Carolingian churches show no structural advance on those reared
in the fourth, fifth, and sixth centuries, while in technique
they are of course infinitely inferior. The church was still
a long aisled building with wooden roofs and as such liable
at any moment to accidental destruction by fire. So long
as this danger was only accidental and consequently infrequent, no very strong impulse existed to urge the builders
towards any more solid and durable construction. This impetus, however, was soon to be supplied. Already before
the death of Charles the Great the Northmen had begun
their pillaging and destructive raids on the northern coasts
of France and during the next century these raids became
more and more severe until few if any parts of the Empire
were immune from their periodic visitation. As a consequence nearly every rural church of any size or accessi-
bility in France was pillaged and burnt, often several times
over. The state of England during the Danish invasions was
repeated and intensified in France, for while, in England, the
emergency produced a strong central government, in France
an effete dynasty failed to take any effective steps to stem
the tide. Just as the monks of Lindisfarne and the body of
their patron St. Cuthbert were driven from home and sent
wandering over the country, so in France the monks of
Noirmoutier and their patron St. Philibert were driven
from their island monastery at the mouth of the Loire, first
inland to the shores of the lake of Grandlieu and finally
right across the country to the banks of the Saone at Tournus.
Even here they were not safe for the Magyar hordes from
central Europe again threatened their existence.

The settling of the Northmen in northern France and
the founding of the Duchy of Normandy in 911 gave that
part of the country immunity from further raids and elsewhere the Northern menace gradually wore itself out. As
a consequence of these more settled conditions, church-
building began again on an extensive scale, but this new

renaissance had other aims than that of Charles the Great and an intelligence, sharpened by adversity, to carry them into effect. From this point indeed emerges in western Europe the idea of a church completely roofed in stone and so immune from the action of fire. Some provinces were more backward than others in pursuing this aim and the methods employed differed in each, but the first steps were now taken on the road which led to the final achievement of the Gothic builders, an entire stone church organically, logically, and structurally complete.

The initiation and course of this development in Normandy must now engage our attention, as this province was the most direct and immediate parent of the Anglo-Norman architecture of the eleventh and twelfth centuries.

The monastic revival which gave the necessary impetus to the architectural revival in Normandy, was largely due to the Italian St. William of Volpiano, Abbot of S. Bénigne at Dijon, who was summoned to Normandy in 1002 by Duke Richard II to reform the monastic life of the Duchy. With him came a colony of Benedictines from Dijon, who were settled at Fécamp. Jumièges also came under his influence and Bernay was founded under his auspices. In spite of these historical connexions with Burgundy and Italy, there is little or no trace of southern influence in the subsequent architecture of Normandy. This architecture is remarkable in more ways than one, for not only was it structurally the most logical of the various contemporary schools of Romanesque but it contributed perhaps more than any other to the early beginnings of that Gothic structure which was the greatest architectural achievement of the Middle Ages. The evolution of Norman architecture in the eleventh century is thus of the highest interest and importance.

Vaulting. It has been claimed by Dr. John Bilson[1] and

---

[1] John Bilson, 'The Beginnings of Gothic Architecture', *Journ. R.I.B.A.*, 3rd ser., vi, pp. 259 and 289, and 'The Norman School and the Beginnings of Gothic Architecture', *Arch. Journ.*, lxxiv, p. 1.

others that, from the beginning, the Norman school envisaged
the construction of a completely stone-vaulted church with
clearstory-lighting, and though this thesis is, in the nature
of the case, hardly capable of proof, it has yet many
points in its favour. The earliest churches, however, show
that their builders had hardly yet defined their intentions
and were still groping for the final solution of the problem,
the main difficulty being the raising of a groined vault
over the main body of the building. This form of vault
(formed by the intersection of a transverse vault with the
main vault in each bay) was the only one, then known,
which permitted lighting by clearstory windows; but it con-
centrated the whole thrust on a series of points in the side
walls instead of distributing it over the whole wall as in
the use of the barrel-vault. In the earliest surviving eleventh-
century church in Normandy at Bernay (Fig. 1),[1] begun
in 1017 and finished perhaps 1040–50, while the aisles had
groined vaults and the apses were semi-domed, there was no
provision at all for a vault in the nave or transept, while
in the choir, shafts were run up the inner face of the piers to
finish ineffectively at the level of the roof-plate. That these
shafts indicate an intention to vault the choir, checked by
inexperience and a fear of its consequences, is certainly
arguable but hardly susceptible of proof, for it might be
argued that they were a mere emphasis of the vertical
division into bays and carried down the lines of the main
roof-trusses to the floor-level. It is not in any case until after
the middle of the century that any surviving church received a stone vault over its main spans. The question is
complicated by the known employment of another form of
partial fire-protection which also demanded the employment of tall wall-shafts. This form, known as the diaphragm-
arch, consisted of dividing the main roof of a building into
sections by masonry gables resting on cross-arches; the effect

---

[1] *Cong. Arch. de France* (Caen), 1908, ii, p. 588, and John Bilson in *Bull. Mon.*,
lxxv (1911), p. 296.

was to confine, to a certain extent, the action of any fire to one section of the roof between the gables and to prevent its rapid spread from end to end of the building. Unfor-

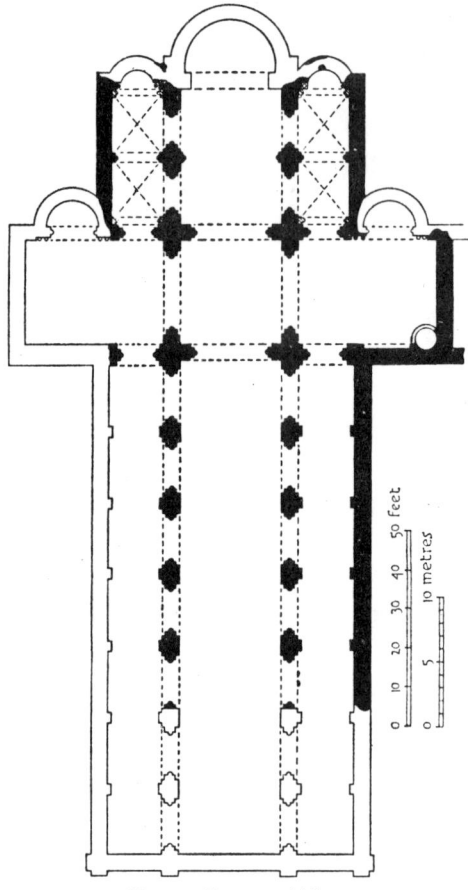

FIG. 1. Bernay Abbey.

tunately no certain example of this construction now survives, though the eighteenth-century illustration of the roofless nave of S. Vigor Priory at Bayeux (Pl. 1),[1] shows the diaphragm-arches as then in existence, and one or two other churches may reasonably be supposed to have formerly

[1] *Mon. Gall.*, ed. Peigné-Delacourt, Pl. CIII.

PLATE 1

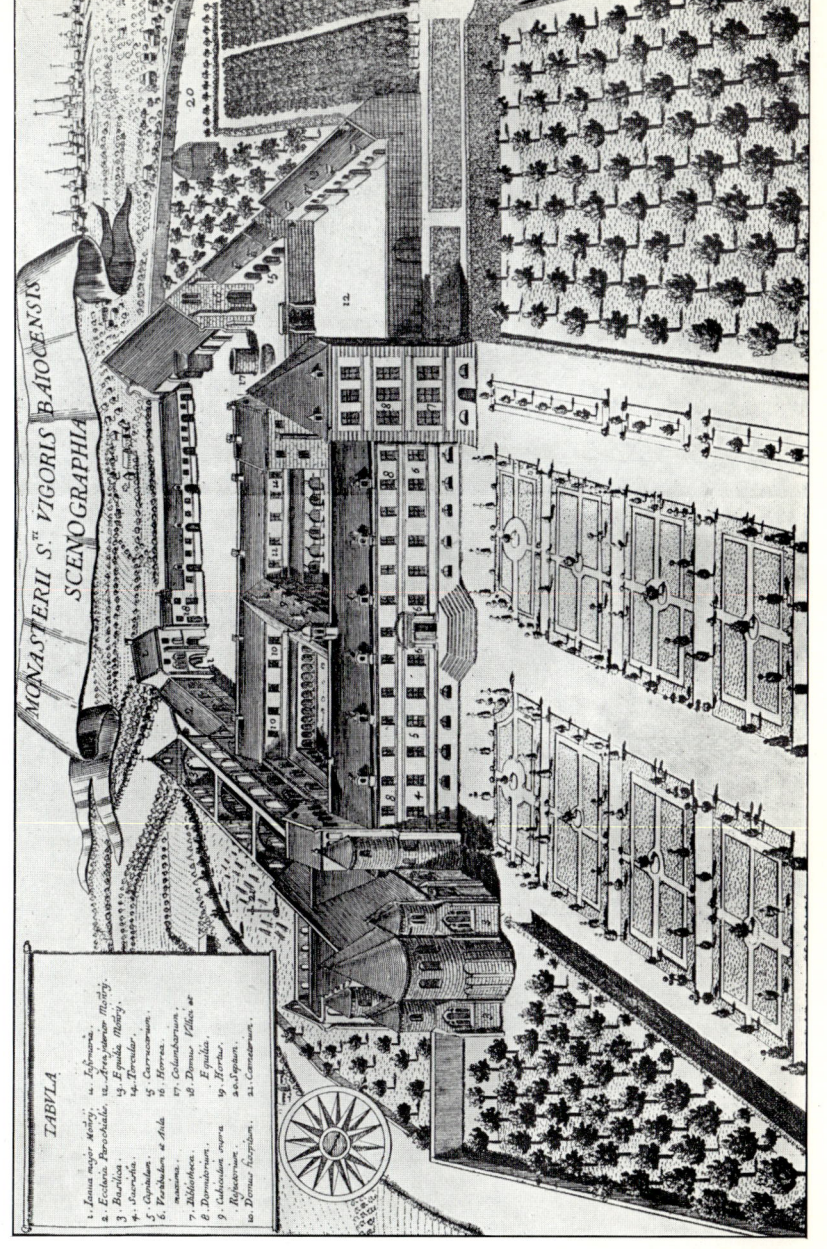

S. VIGOR PRIORY, BAYEUX, *in the 18th century*

possessed them.[1] Of these the most important for our purpose is the nave of Jumièges (1040–67). Here (Fig. 2) a system of double-bays is adopted, that is to say heavy piers of compound form, alternate with cylindrical piers of much slighter construction; the compound piers have wall-shafts carried up to the base of the clearstory, above which are the marks of the removal of a wall or shaft running up to the roof-level. There are certain, but by no means conclusive, reasons[2] for assuming that this arrangement implies the former existence of diaphragm-arches, which do not seem to have been carried across between each bay of any building, but only between alternate bays. At S. Étienne, Caen,[3] on the other hand, the original clearstory of the nave had four closely grouped lights in the middle of a double bay, as though for the erection of a vault, over the double bay which at this date (1064–73) would have been a very early instance outside Italy. Here again, however, there is an instance of infirmity of purpose, for an intermediate wall-shaft is carried up to the base of the original clearstory beyond which point it was impossible to carry it owing to the close grouping of the windows above.

Other early churches of Normandy, besides the choir of Bernay, had these wall-shafts carried up to the roof-level, between each bay, as in the nave at Mont-S.-Michel[4]

[1] A plausible case has been made out for them at Cerisy la Forêt, *Cong. Arch. de France* (Caen), ii, p. 545.
[2] The nave received a plaster vault in 1692 springing from the existing capitals and if, as has been assumed, the wall-shafts originally ran up to the roof-level, the cutting back of the whole of the upper part would have been a waste of labour as all above the vault would be hidden from view. On the other hand the removal of a cross-wall may well have been necessary. The intention of the designers to raise a high stone vault over the building is improbable as it implies a groined vault over a double bay, at a date when, so far as we know, no one in Normandy had ventured even to raise a similar vault over a single bay and furthermore the lofty clearstory has no possible abutment for such a thrust. R. Martin du Gard, *L'Abbaye de Jumièges* (1909) and L.-M. Michon, and R. Martin du Gard, *L'Abbaye de Jumièges* (1927).
[3] *Cong. Arch. de France* (Caen), i, p. 20, and G. Bonet, *L'Abbaye de S. Étienne de Caen* (1868).
[4] P. Gout, *Le Mont-S.-Michel*, 1910; C. H. Besnard, *Le Mont-S.-Michel*.

(*c.* 1040) and S. Gervais, Falaise[1] (late eleventh century), but in neither case was a stone vault ever constructed upon them.

The actual raising of a groined stone vault over the main span was finally accomplished in three churches of the age of William the Conqueror—the choir of the Trinité, Caen[2] (1062–6), the choir of the church of S. Nicolas (Fig. 3)[3] in the same town (*c.* 1083), and Notre Dame sur l'eau, Domfront[4] (*c.* 1050–60). From this point onwards the Norman school took the foremost place among the north French schools. Its type was not only more stabilized than that of the others, but all the component parts of the building were designed to perform each its own functional purpose in the general scheme.

Internal Elevation. The internal elevation of these eleventh-century Norman churches indicates two very different schemes of proportion; in the one and this perhaps the earlier, the main arcades are far taller than the triforium (sometimes more than double the height); while in the second the two stages are of nearly equal height. The first type may be seen at Bernay, Jumièges, and S. Nicolas, Caen, while the second is exemplified at S. Étienne, Caen, and Cerisy.

The triforium story, itself, was an innovation, or rather the re-introduction of a feature, which was absent from the basilican churches of the Carolingian age. It was the logical result of a vaulted aisle having a steep pent-roof of timber above it. For this arrangement necessitated a considerable stretch of walling between the main arcade and the clearstory, which might either remain blank or, if any use was to be made of the space between the aisle-vault and its roof, must be pierced by openings from the church itself to provide light. The triforium opening varied greatly; in the choir of Bernay it consisted of twin round-headed openings,

[1] *Cong. Arch. de France* (Caen), i, p. 373.
[2] *Ibid.*, i, p. 4.   [3] *Ibid.*, i, p. 54.
[4] V. Ruprich-Robert, *L'Architecture normande*, i, Pls. 8, 21, and 22.

at Jumièges of a large arch with three equal sub-arches, at S. Étienne, Caen, of a single open arch of greater width than the main arch below, at Cerisy of a large arch with two sub-arches, and at Mont-S.-Michel of two such arches. The triforium passage at Jumièges was roofed with groined vaults a proceeding which at a later date was often replaced by barrel or half-barrel vaults or simply by butting arches as a support to the high vault of the main building. The vaults at Jumièges, however, would have been of little value for such a purpose as they were covered by a steep pent-roof which raised the clearstory high above them.

The clearstory commonly had a single window in each bay sometimes enclosed in a triple arcade as at Cerisy or a quadruple arcade to the double bay as at S. Étienne, Caen.

In the transept at Bernay may be noted the partial introduction of the clearstory wall-passage, which was a distinctive feature of the Norman school, and was very persistent in English work. The placing of the floor of this wall-passage well below the level of the window-sills rendered possible a great improvement in the internal proportions of the building.

The main piers of some of the earlier churches (e.g. Mont-S.-Michel) were square with one attached shaft on each face, at Bernay the piers are compound and at Jumièges compound piers alternated with cylindrical columns, forming a very definite double bay, an arrangement which was to be copied in an important group of English churches. The arches were invariably round and of plain square orders or arch-rings, sometimes with a half-round roll or moulding on the soffit of the arch. From the middle of the century the compound piers become more complicated both by the addition of further offsets to the responds of the main arcade and by more commonly setting the wall-shafts against a pilaster on the other two sides. The orders of the main arches are also increased in

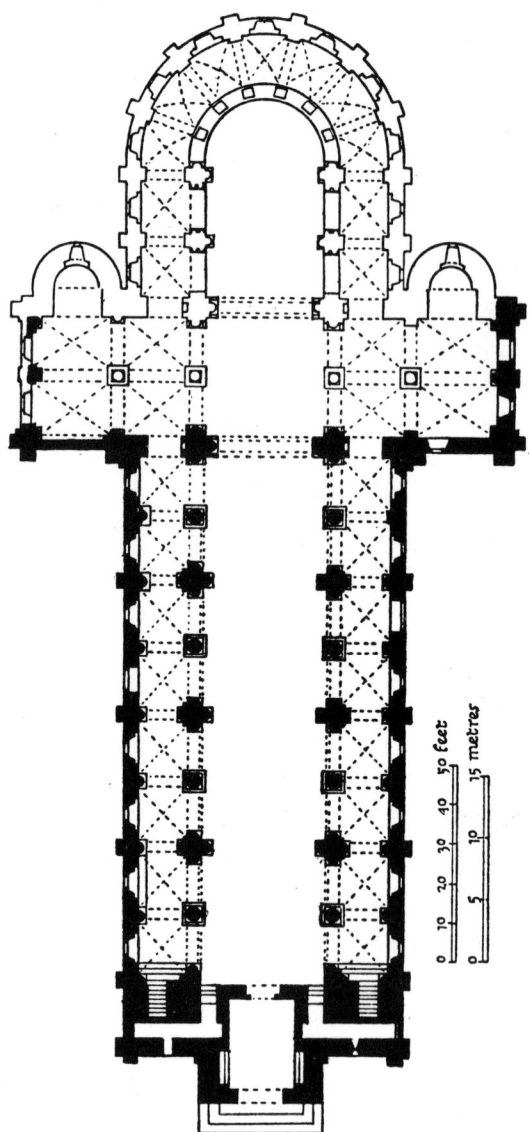

Fig. 2. Jumièges Abbey.

number to correspond with the piers and begin to receive a roll-moulding on the edge instead of the plain square orders and soffit-roll of the earlier examples.

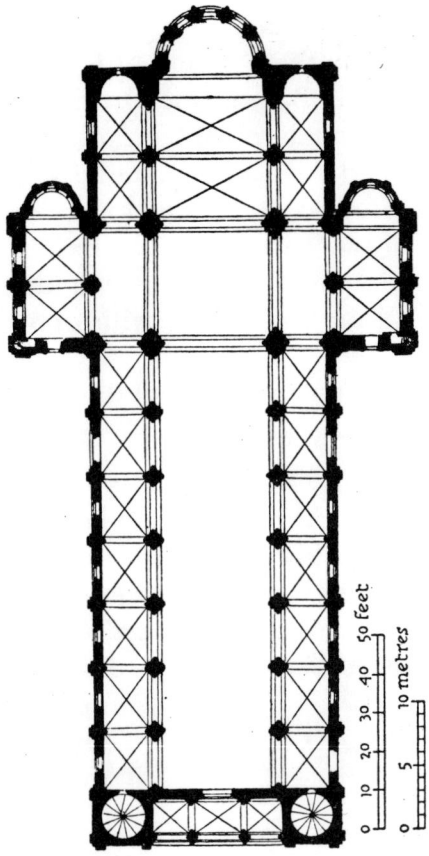

FIG. 3. S. Nicolas, Caen.

Plan. Norman Romanesque has been divided into two minor schools associated geographically with the two centres, Rouen and Caen. The churches of the latter group present a greater uniformity of plan, and furthermore, are more generally preserved than those in and near the capital of the Duchy. Throughout Normandy, however, the planning of the major churches displays less variety, and the general structure a greater cohesion than is observable in most of the other French schools.

The typical Norman plan owes its component parts to a variety of sources which have been considered by the late M. Lefèvre-Pontalis under the name of the Benedictine plan[1] This, which there seems little reason to connect particularly with the Benedictine Order, was not confined to Normandy, but, on the other hand, was there reproduced with a general and particular uniformity which render it typical of the province.[2] It consists of an apsidal choir, nearly always of two bays, side-aisles terminating in apses, transept with an apsidal chapel in each arm, a tower over the crossing and an aisled nave with or without western towers.

The eleventh-century churches of this type which survive in whole or in part are as follows:

Bernay Abbey (Fig. 1)	1017–c. 1050.
Bayeux Cathedral[3] (crypt)	*ante* 1049 (?).
Caen La Trinité Abbey	1062–6.
,, S. Nicolas (Fig. 3)	begun c. 1083.
Evreux S. Taurin Abbey[4]	late eleventh-century.
Cerisy la Forêt Abbey	second half of the eleventh century.
Montivilliers Abbey[5]	last third of the eleventh century.
Lessay Abbey[6]	end of the eleventh century.

[1] E. Lefèvre-Pontalis, 'Le Plan des églises romanes bénédictines', *Bull. Mon.*, lxxvi (1912), p. 439.

[2] The excavations of Professor K. Conant at Cluny seem likely to show that this plan may have been that adopted in the second church at Cluny (consecrated 981). If so the plan may have been introduced into Normandy by the mission of St. William of Volpiano, whose reform was of Cluniac inspiration.

[3] J. Vallery-Radot, *Bayeux Cathedral.* It cannot be said to be proved that this east end was not surrounded by an ambulatory.

[4] G. Bonnenfant, *L'Église S. Taurin* (1926).

[5] *Cong. Arch. de France* (Rouen), p. 476.

[6] *Ibid.* (Caen), i, p. 244.

To these may be added Mont-S.-Michel Abbey, S. Étienne Abbey, Caen (1064–73), and S. Ouen Abbey, Rouen[1] (begun 1056 or 1066), of which the form of the east end is not certainly known and Lyre Abbey[2] rebuilt about 1150 but preserving, in all probability, the plan of the church begun *c.* 1050.[3]

The component parts of this plan are of varied derivation, thus the triple apse termination of the east end appears from the eighth century onwards in churches of Rome and Italy. The transept with the projecting choir or presbytery was contributed by the Carolingian architects, and the cruciform church with three eastern apses can be seen in the late ninth-century additions to the church of S. Philibert de Grandlieu (Déols).[4] A still closer parallel has recently been excavated under the church of S. Solenne (the cathedral) at Blois;[5] it is ascribed to the early part of the tenth century, but here while the crossing is present there is no evidence of the projecting transepts. A peculiar feature, more common in the Norman school than elsewhere, is the provision of the gallery across part or the whole of the arms of the transept. Something of the sort appears to have existed at S. Solenne, and was present also at S. Remi at Reims[6] (*c.* 1039–45). In Normandy, this gallery extended over the whole transept, up to the crossing, at Jumièges Abbey and Bayeux Cathedral, and in numerous other churches it existed over the projecting part of the transept only.[7] It is generally, if not always, accompanied by an apsidal eastern chapel

[1] A. Masson, *L'Église S. Ouen de Rouen*, p. 29.
[2] G. Guéry, *Hist. de l'abbaye de Lyre* (1917), Plan, p. 530. The building no longer exists.
[3] A number of later churches, including S. Georges de Boscherville Abbey (*c.* 1123), S. Gabriel Priory, and S. Vigor Priory, Bayeux, followed the same plan.
[4] R. de Lasteyrie, *Mém. Acad. des Inscriptions et Belles-Lettres*, xxxviii, 2, p. 1.
[5] Dr. Lesueur, 'Les fouilles de la cathédrale de Blois,' *Bull. Mon.*, lxxxix (1930), p. 435.
[6] *Cong. Arch. de France* (Rheims), i, p. 85.
[7] E.g. Caen (S. Étienne and S. Nicolas), Cerisy la Forêt, S. Taurin, Évreux, S. Ouen, Rouen, and S. Georges de Boscherville.

of two storys, and formed the means of approach to the upper chapel.

It is unfortunate that, with the exceptions of Rouen and perhaps Bayeux and Évreux,[1] the plan of the eastern parts of none of the early Norman cathedrals is known, and it may be argued that the greater churches exhibited more diversity in planning than is indicated by the examples cited above. Thus the church of S. Ouen, Rouen (begun 1056 or 1066) had two apsidal chapels of differing projection in each arm of the transept, but the form of the choir and its aisles is unknown. The Cathedral of Rouen[2] (begun c. 1025–30) and the abbey church of Jumièges[3] (built between 1040 and 1067) certainly had an ambulatory (Fig. 2) round the main apse and in the former case remains of one of the radiating chapels have also been found.

In view of the equal popularity of the three-apse plan, and the ambulatory plan in England immediately after the Conquest, some consideration must be given to the origin of the latter form which seems to have made only an exceptional appearance in Normandy. In the neighbouring provinces, towards the south and bordering on the middle Loire, the ambulatory plan, combined with a series of radiating chapels, was rather the rule than the exception at this same period. The earliest example, in this district, which can be definitely dated, would appear to be the church of the abbey of La Couture at Le Mans,[4] built late in the tenth century and which still partly survives. It was followed by the rebuilding (after the fire of 997) at S. Martin at Tours,[5] S. Aignan at Orléans[6] (begun 1029), the abbey of Beaulieu

[1] Fossey, *Mon. de la cath. d'Évreux* (1898).

[2] The remains of the ambulatory, suggested by Dr. John Bilson in *Bull. Mon.* (1927), p. 251, have recently (1931) been found by M. Georges Lanfry, who had previously established the existence of the ambulatory at Jumièges.

[3] *Bull. Mon.* lxxxvii (1928), p. 127.

[4] *Cong. Arch. de France* (Angers et Saumur), i. p. 281.

[5] R. de Lasteyrie, *Mém. de l'Acad. des Inscriptions et Belles-lettres*, xxxiv, Pt. I, p. 1.

[6] *Cong. Arch. de France* (Orléans), 1930, p. 52.

les Loches,[1] and Chartres Cathedral[2] all dating from early in the eleventh century.[3] It has, of late years, been the custom, following the lead of the late Comte R. de Lasteyrie, to derive the immediate origin of the ambulatory plan from the early tenth-century (903–19) church of S. Martin at Tours, which this author identified with the broader and more massive foundations underlying the walls of the early eleventh-century church above referred to. This conclusion is open to the gravest doubts, for not only is it improbable that two churches, differing in date by a century, should follow the same plan, but the divergence in lines between the two sets of foundations is hardly greater than that commonly found in medieval buildings between the foundations and the superstructure of the same building.

There actually survive, elsewhere in France, two earlier examples of the ambulatory plan than those cited above, and both these display primitive features which accord well with their date, and are unrepresented in the supposed earlier church at Tours. The earlier of these examples, at Clermont-Ferrand Cathedral,[4] begun in 946, had a curious depressed apse and four square-ended radiating chapels; the second at the abbey of Tournus,[5] dating probably from 980, has a semi-circular ambulatory and three square-ended chapels. So far then, as type is concerned, it would appear that the ambulatory plan travelled northwards, and had reached Normandy at any rate by 1030, though here its employment, so far as we know, seems to have been infrequent. The favour in which it was held in England

[1] *Ibid.* (Angers), ii, p. 91.
[2] E. Lefèvre-Pontalis in *Bull. Mon.*, lxvi (1903), p. 381, and R. Merlet, *La Cathédrale de Chartres*.
[3] Other eleventh-century examples may be cited at Vendôme (dedicated 1040), S. Benoît-sur-Loire, S. Julien-du-Pré, Le Mans, and probably S. Mexime Chinon.
[4] H. du Ranquet, *La Cathédrale de Clermont-Ferrand*, p. 33, and in *Bull. Mon.*, 1909, p. 311. The east end of this church is compared with that of S. Aignan, Orléans, by a contemporary of the building of the latter, *Cong. Arch. de France* (Orléans) 1930, p. 53.
[5] *Cong. Arch. de France* (Dijon), 1929, p. 368.

immediately after the Conquest may thus be due either to the earlier Norman models or to a more direct influence from farther south. Some support is given to the latter theory by the fact that the monks who colonized the Conqueror's abbey of Battle and indeed are said to have had to do with the actual building, came from Marmoutier[1] by Tours, in a district in which the ambulatory plan was well established, and the church at Battle was probably the first in England in which this plan was adopted.

The early Norman churches seem always to have been provided with a central tower built on equal arches over the crossing. At Jumièges and Domfront this rose two stages above the walls of the church and one clear stage above the high roofs. The presence of a pair of western towers depended on the relative importance of the church. They were present at any rate in most of the cathedrals and in the greater abbey churches. The least altered example may be seen at Jumièges.

Ornament and Details. Carved ornament in early Norman churches is almost entirely confined to the capitals of columns and shafts, and here the nearly universal form adopted is the carved volute at the angles; sometimes one or two rows of simple leaves are added below,[2] in remote imitation of the classic Corinthian form, and very occasionally the body of the capital is carved with crude designs[3] or even figures. The execution of this carving is quite barbaric and there is no evidence that the Norman masons or carvers of that age ever achieved or even attempted any higher or more ambitious form of plastic art. The cubical capital, not of the cushion-type, makes a very occasional appearance in Normandy and it was obviously not native to the province.

The base-mouldings generally conform to one of three

---

[1] No remains of the eleventh-century church exist at Marmoutier itself but the plan, as we have seen, was normal in the district.

[2] E.g. Bayeux (crypt), Caen, S. Trinité (crypt), Caen, S. Nicolas (narthex).

[3] E.g. Bernay.

types: (*a*) the classical Attic base, rudely rendered;[1] (*b*) the flat double hollow-chamfer;[2] and (*c*) the hollow-moulding with a roll below it.[3]

[1] This is to be found at Caen, S. Trinité, Bayeux Cathedral (crypt), and Rouen Cathedral (crypt).
[2] This is exemplified at Caen, S. Étienne, S. Trinité, and S. Nicolas, Jumièges, Mont-S.-Michel, Rouen, S. Ouen, Lessay, and Fécamp.
[3] This is found at Caen, S. Trinité, and Lessay.

Chapter II

ANGLO-NORMAN CHURCHES

ONE of the most immediate results of the Norman Conquest was the reorganization of the English Church. A council held at Windsor in 1070 deprived the primate Stigand and several of his suffragans of their sees and on the death of the other Saxon bishops they were immediately replaced by Normans. Thus within ten years of the Conquest all the English sees were held by Normans or other foreigners with the solitary exception of Worcester, where the Saxon Wulfstan still maintained his position. In addition to this the same process took place in all the greater monasteries then existing and numerous new monasteries were founded by William and his chief followers. A council held at Windsor, in 1072, decreed the removal of rural sees to the major towns in their dioceses, a decree which was repeated at the council of London in 1075. This led to the transfer of the see at Dorchester to Lincoln, Sherborne to Old Sarum, Selsey to Chichester, Elmham to Thetford and eventually to Norwich, Wells to Bath, and Lichfield to Chester.

The new Norman prelates, drawn largely from the then flourishing monasteries of Normandy, were impatient of the lax practices and somewhat inchoate architecture of the Saxon Church, and hastened to reform both the one and the other to the Norman model, and even without the excuse of the transference of the see, the reconstruction of the majority of the English cathedrals was undertaken within a few years. So universal and so contagious was the practice that the sole surviving Saxon bishop Wulfstan felt himself compelled to conform to the general fashion and—as he is reputed to have put it—destroying the works of his forefathers, laboured to heap up stones.

The coincidence of this unrivalled opportunity with the progressiveness and vigour of the Norman school of Romanesque, produced a renaissance of architecture in England, which forms one of the great epochs of architectural history. The dimensions of the parent stock were soon outstripped and the Anglo-Norman builder early showed a capacity for progress and even originality which placed this country in the forefront of architectural development.

The Anglo-Norman churches of the first generation after the Conquest form a nearly homogeneous class of building which is indivisible into geographical schools and is in most of its structural features a reproduction of the Norman Romanesque of the continent. Occasionally, as in certain churches of the west country, we seem to trace some influence from farther afield, or here and there a survival of native Saxon ideas. In decorative forms, however, the kinship with continental Norman is not so marked; thus the volute-capital, almost universally used in Normandy, is less frequent in England, its place being taken by the cushion-capital. In plan too, the Anglo-Norman architects showed far more diversity of choice than those of Normandy had done; a few of the earliest churches follow strictly the lines of the continental Norman work, but there is an almost immediate break away both in plan and dimensions, which resulted in a more ambitious type of building and eventually in the production, at Durham, of the foremost monument of the school.

Before proceeding to the consideration of the general characteristics of these buildings, it will be necessary to give a summary account of the most important English churches of the first period, that is to say of the reigns of the Conqueror and William Rufus. These accounts are intended only to indicate the recorded dates of the buildings, their general form, and extant remains. They are divided into two series following the two main types of plan, (*a*) the three-apse type, and (*b*) the apse and ambulatory type; the former, as we have seen, follows the most common Norman practice and the latter the practice more common farther south.

The geographical distribution of the two types reveals nothing, such neighbouring buildings as the two great churches at Canterbury, Winchester and Christchurch, Norwich and Ely, exhibiting the opposing types of plan. Neither, except perhaps for the solitary exception of Battle, can anything be learned from the place of origin of the ecclesiastics for whom the buildings were erected; the choice must have been decided by unknown factors, of which one may have been the place of origin of the master-mason. It may, however, be observed that the three-apse plan is much less common in the western parts of the country than in the midlands and the east, though Old Sarum, Shaftesbury, and probably Exeter, at a later date, provide examples of the more unusual form.

A. THE THREE-APSE TYPE.

(1) *Westminster.* Of the Confessor's abbey church[1] at Westminster (Benedictine), begun about 1045-50 and consecrated in 1065, little is certainly known except concerning the eastern arm, and the west end. The lower part of the north wall of the choir and part of the main apse have been found under the presbytery and the Confessor's chapel of the later building. The choir consisted of two bays with solid side walls and an apse. That the crossing and transepts occupied the same position as the later crossing and transepts is indicated by the surviving remains of the early monastic buildings. Recent excavations[2] (1930) have laid bare the western part of the south arcade of the nave, and the south-west tower. It would appear that the nave was of six double bays, after the manner of Jumièges, with alternate cruciform and square piers.

---

[1] Dean Armitage Robinson in *Arch.,* lxii, p. 81. *Roy. Com. on Hist. Mons., London, Westminster Abbey.*   [2] *Arch.* lxxxiii.

(2) *Canterbury Cathedral*[1] (Benedictine). The Saxon cathedral was damaged and partly destroyed by fire in 1067, and Archbishop Lanfranc[2] built the new cathedral (Fig. 16) in seven years starting in 1070 or 1071. The east arm of this building was replaced by a very much larger choir begun by Prior Ernulf[3] (1096–1107) and completed by Prior Conrad (1108–26). This extension was consecrated in 1130.[4] Lanfranc's church consisted of a choir of two bays presumably with an apse, aisles also terminating in apses, transepts with galleries over the projecting parts and eastern chapels of two storys, and a nave of nine bays including the two west towers. Considerable portions of the two transepts remain, though much concealed by later work. Fragments also survive in the lower parts of the nave. The east end has never been satisfactorily determined; excavations made in 1895, revealed a foundation with a curved east face at the end of the early north aisle, and a raft of rubble of indeterminate form was found on the site of the main apse. There appears to have been a crypt under the choir of which some remains may exist at the west end of the present crypt.

(3) *Lincoln Cathedral* (secular)[5] was begun by Bishop Remi of Fécamp in 1072–3[6] and was consecrated in 1092,[7] when, according to Henry of Huntingdon,[8] it was finished. The only surviving part above ground is the west front with its two towers, with inserted twelfth-century doorways and added superstructure to the towers. The plan of the rest of the church was recovered by excavation at various dates. It consisted of a choir of three bays with an apse and solid side walls, choir-aisles terminating in apses, square externally,

---

[1] R. Willis, *The Architectural Hist. of Canterbury Cathedral.*
[2] Eadmer, Vita Bregwini, *Ang. Sac.*, ii, p. 188.
[3] William of Malmesbury, *Gesta Pont.* (Rolls Ser.), p. 138.
[4] *Gervase of Canterbury (Act. Pont.)* (Rolls Ser.), ii, p. 383.
[5] John Bilson, 'The plan of the first cathedral church of Lincoln', *Arch.*, lxii, p. 543.
[6] Dugdale, *Mon. Ang.* (1830), vi, p. 1270.
[7] *Giraldus Cambrensis, Vita S. Remigii* (Rolls Ser.), vii, p. 21.
[8] *Hist. Ang.* (Rolls. Ser.), p. 216.

transepts with a short eastern aisle and galleries to the transept, and a nave of ten bays excluding the towers. After a fire in 1141 the nave was covered with stone vaults[1] by Bishop Alexander (1123–47) and various alterations made to the west front.

(4) *Old Sarum* (secular). The Cathedral of Old Sarum[2] was begun by Bishop Hermann[3] between the years 1075 and 1078. It was finished by his successor Osmund and consecrated in 1092.[4] The church (Fig. 4) was subsequently enlarged eastwards by Bishop Roger[5] (1103–39). The first church consisted of a choir of two bays and an apse, side-aisles, square transepts with eastern apses, and a nave of eight bays. The solid side walls of the choir seem to have been continued westward as far as the middle of the transept, where they were met by the arcades of the nave. There was thus no provision for a central tower and the square transepts with sleeper walls across their inner faces may well have supported transeptal towers, though the sleeper walls would serve equally well for the bases of the columns which supported a gallery in so many early Norman churches. The plan of the church was recovered by excavation in 1912–13, and the walls are now marked out on the surface of the ground.

(5) *St. Albans.*[6] The abbey church (Fig. 5) of St. Albans (Benedictine) was begun and apparently finished by Abbot Paul of Caen[7] between the years 1077 and 1088, but it was not consecrated until 1115.[8] It is built almost entirely of Roman brick with a little re-use of Saxon material. The plan consisted of a choir of four bays with an apse and solid side walls, aisles presumably with eastern apses, transepts each

---

[1] *Giraldus Cambrensis, Vita S. Remigii* (Rolls Ser.).
[2] Reports of the excavations of Old Sarum, *Proc. Soc. Ants.*, xxv, p. 93; xxvi, p. 100; xxvii, p. 230.
[3] William of Malmesbury, *Gesta Pont.* (Rolls Ser.), p. 183.
[4] *Simeon of Durham* (Rolls Ser.), ii, p. 219.
[5] William of Malmesbury, *Gesta Reg. Ang.* (Rolls Ser.), ii, p. 484.
[6] C. R. Peers and W. Page in *V.C.H., Herts.*, ii, p. 483.
[7] *Gesta Abbat.* (Rolls Ser.), i, pp. 52 and 53.   [8] *Ibid.*, p. 71.

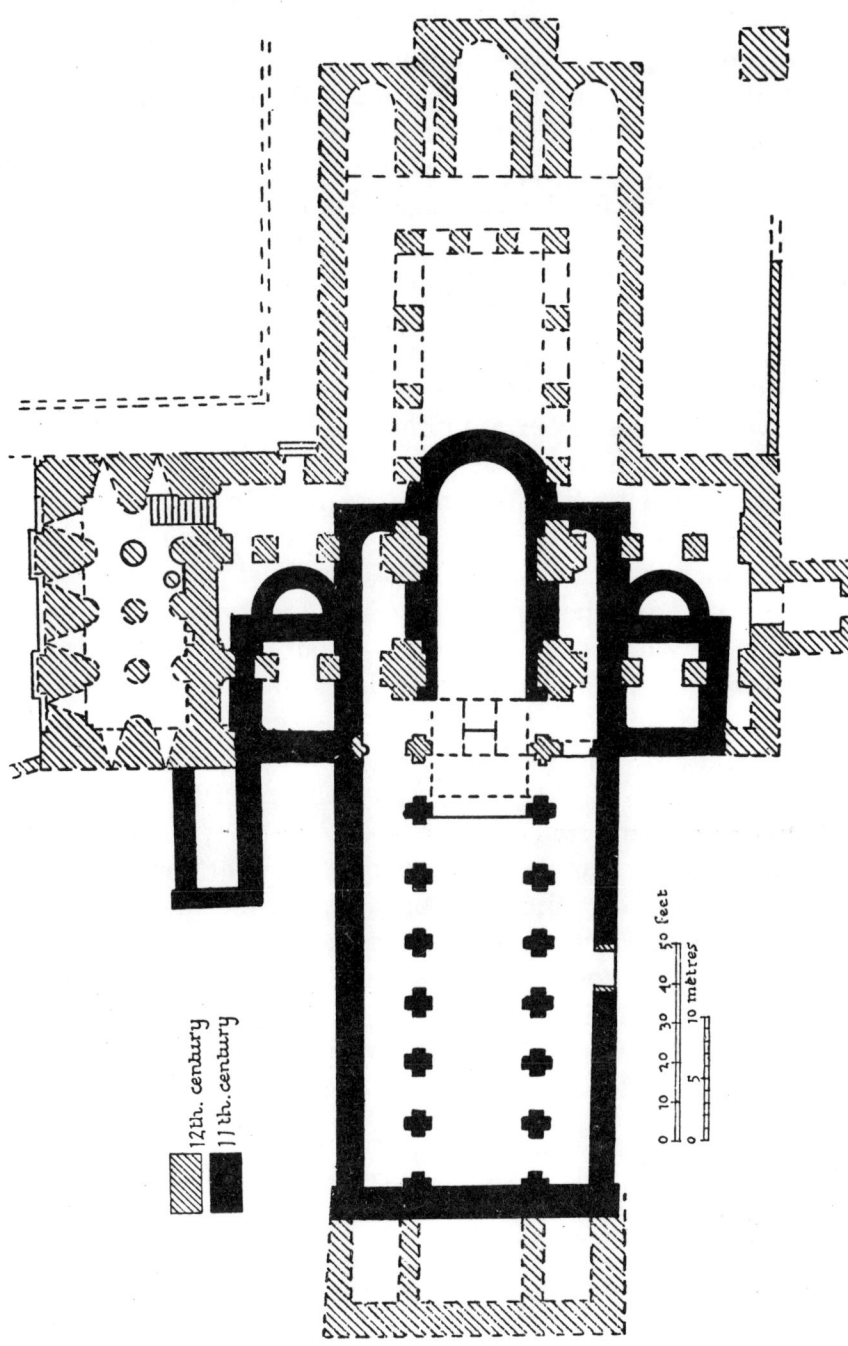

12th. century

11th. century

0 10 20 30 40 50 feet
0   5   10 metres

Fig. 4. OLD SARUM CATHEDRAL.

with two apsidal chapels set in echelon and a nave and aisles probably of ten bays.[1] Considerable portions survive of all these parts except the eastern apses, but some indications of the main apse were found in 1845.[2] The transept, crossing (Pl. 9), central tower and nearly all of the north side of the nave survive largely unaltered except by modern restoration.

(6) *Rochester*. Rochester Cathedral[3] (Benedictine) was begun by Bishop Gundulf shortly after his consecration in 1077; with the aid of Archbishop Lanfranc it is said to have been completed in a few years.[4] It seems more probable, however, that the nave was finished rather later. The plan of the early church is at present undetermined. The form suggested by Sir William Hope rests on little or no evidence and is neither reasonable nor probable. Dr. Fairweather has recently shown that a normal plan, similar to that of Lanfranc's church at Canterbury is quite a possible lay out for the site, but without excavation it is impossible to prove it. In any case the existing crypt (Pl. 26) with the foundations of a square east end, assigned to Gundulf, must belong to a later extension, perhaps the work of Bishop Ernulf (1115–24), who began the earlier extension at Canterbury.

The surviving remains of the early church at Rochester are thus very scanty, including only parts of the outer walls of the nave aisles and perhaps the core of some of the nave piers. The north tower, formerly detached and now ruined, is also part of Gundulf's work.

(7) *Ely*. Ely Abbey church[5] (Benedictine) later cathedral, was begun[6] by Abbot Simeon (1081–93), brother of Bishop

[1] W. Page in *Arch.*, lvi, p. 21.
[2] Buckler, *Abbey Church of St. Alban*, p. 59.
[3] Sir Wm. St. J. Hope, 'The Arch. Hist. of the Cath. Church of Rochester', in *Arch. Cant.*, xxiii, p. 194; Dr. F. H. Fairweather in *Arch. Journ.*, lxxxvi, p. 187.
[4] *Textus Roffen.* (ed. Hearne), p. 143; and Wharton, *Ang. Sac.*, ii, p. 280.
[5] D. J. Stewart, *On the Architectural Hist. of Ely Cath.*, 1868; T. D. Atkinson, *The Architectural Hist. of the Monastery of Ely*, 1933; and *The Builder*, 1892, i, p. 266.
[6] *Lib. Eliensis* (Ang. Christiana), p. 253.

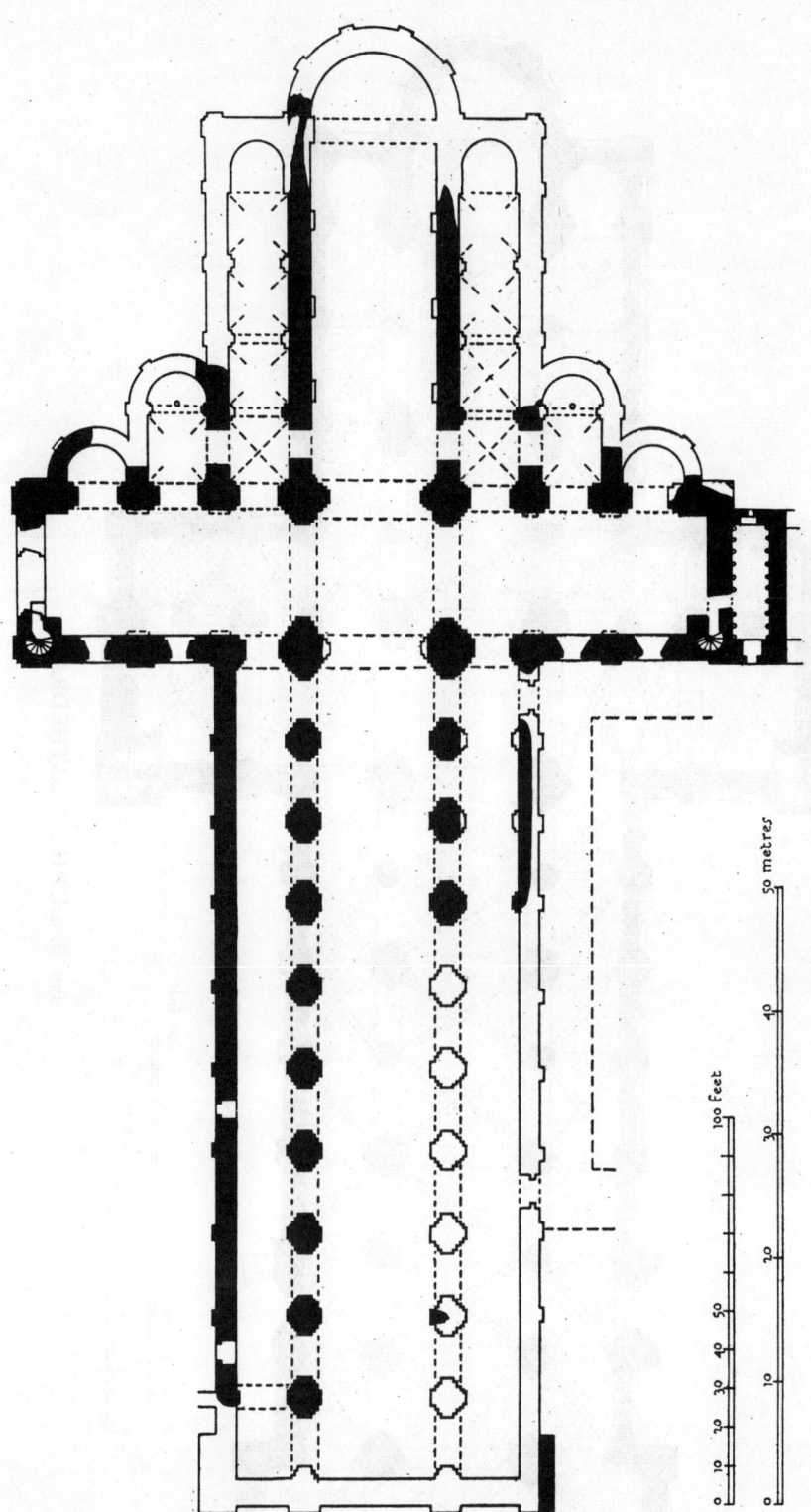

100 Feet

50 metres

FIG. 5. ST. ALBANS ABBEY.

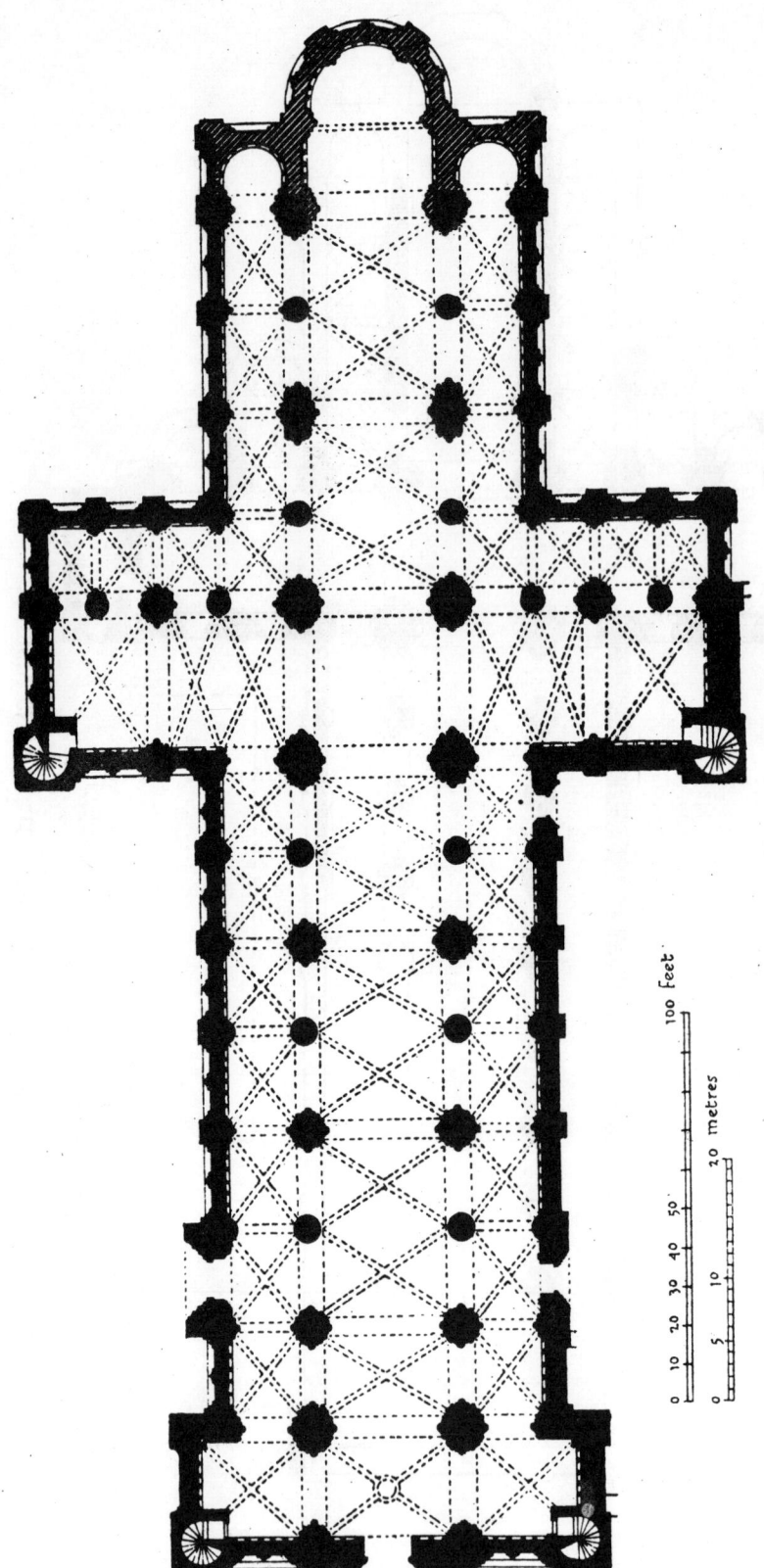

Fig. 6. DURHAM CATHEDRAL.

Walkelin of Winchester, and Abbot Richard (1100–7) worked at it so long as he was abbot.[1] That he finished even the greater part of it is unlikely, and it was not until the time of Bishop Geoffrey Ridel (1174–89) that the 'new work towards the west' (west transept), with the west tower was completed.[2] The church originally consisted of a choir of four bays with an apse,[3] aisles perhaps terminating in square ends, transepts with east and west aisles and a nave (Pl. 3) of thirteen bays with a western transept, tower and flanking apsidal chapels. The building survives except for the choir with its aisles, the crossing and adjacent piers, and the north arm of the west transept.

(8) *York, St. Mary's Abbey.* York Abbey as a Benedictine house was due to certain monks from Whitby. The church was begun in 1089[4] when William Rufus laid the first stone. The plan of the east end of this church has been recovered by excavation,[5] and was similar in arrangement to that of St. Albans Abbey. The choir, however, was probably of two bays only, with an apse, flanking apsidal chapels, square-ended externally, and two apsidal chapels in each transept, set in echelon. The nave was probably of eight bays like its successor.

(9) *Durham* (Fig. 6). Durham Cathedral[6] (Benedictine) was begun by Bishop William of St. Calais in 1093.[7] At the accession of Bishop Flambard the building had advanced as far as the nave[8] and at his death in 1128[9] the nave was carried up as far as the roof. By 1133[10] the building was

---

[1] Wharton, *Ang. Sac.*, i, p. 613, and *Lib. Eli.*, i, p. 288.

[2] Wharton, *Ang. Sac.*, i, p. 631.

[3] The foundations are described by Prof. Willis in D. J. Stewart, *op. cit.*, p. 24. An ambulatory was looked for and found not to exist. Across the north aisle ran a wall level with the sleeper-wall across the chord of the main apse.

[4] Dugdale, *Mon. Ang.*, iii, p. 546.

[5] John Bilson in *Arch. Journ.*, lxiii, p. 114 (plan by W. H. Brierley).

[6] John Bilson, 'On the recent discoveries at the east end of Durham Cathedral', in *Arch. Journ.*, liii, pl.; 'Durham Cathedral and the chronology of its vaults', in *Ibid.*, lxxix, p. 101. *V.C.H.*, *Durham*, ii, p. 96.

[7] *Symeon of Durham* (Rolls Ser.), i, pp. 128–9.

[8] *Ibid.*, i, p. 139.   [9] *Ibid.*, i, pp. 139–40.   [10] *Ibid.*, i, p. 141.

completed. It is the most complete and least altered of all the early Anglo-Norman churches and may be considered the finest, and organically the most perfect achievement of the Anglo-Norman school. The church (Frontispiece and Pls. 5, 6, and 13) consists of an aisled choir of four bays (or two double bays), transepts with an eastern aisle, and nave of eight bays including the two western towers. The extreme east end is the only part not now existing above ground; this consisted of a main apse with a narrow bay to the west and side apses, finished square externally.

(10) *Christchurch.* The collegiate church of Christchurch, Twynham[1] (Hants) (afterwards a Priory of Austin Canons), was begun by Dean Ralph Flambard (Bishop of Durham 1099–1128) towards the close of the eleventh century. It was unfinished in 1100[2] and was completed by Dean Gilbert de Dousgunels (1128–?). The church consisted of a choir of three bays presumably with an apse, side-aisles, square-ended externally, transepts each with an apsidal chapel (Pl. 15), and a nave of eight bays. Under the east end of the choir and the outer bays and chapels of the transepts are three small crypts. There is evidence of the design to erect galleries over the whole area of the transepts, up to the crossing.[3] These were intended to be supported on stone vaults. The eastern crypt shows the extent of the eastern arm, though the superstructure has been entirely rebuilt at a later date. The transepts and nave survive largely intact.

A few other churches of the second rank, belonging to this type, must also be mentioned. In the case of Whitby and Eye nothing is now standing above ground and at Blyth the plan of the east arm has been recovered by excavation.

---

[1] C. R. Peers in *V.C.H., Hants,* v, p. 101.
[2] Dugdale, *Mon. Ang.,* vi (1830), p. 303. Flambard is said to have destroyed the earlier church, and nine others which were in the cemetery.
[3] This evidence is largely confined to the north transept, and there is some doubt if the gallery was actually erected over the south half of the transept, though no doubt this was the intended arrangement. The evidence in the south transept has been largely obliterated by fifteenth-century alterations.

century (Fig. 8). The east end, recovered by excavation, reproduced the seven apses in echelon of the parent abbey of St. Albans. The nave is still standing.

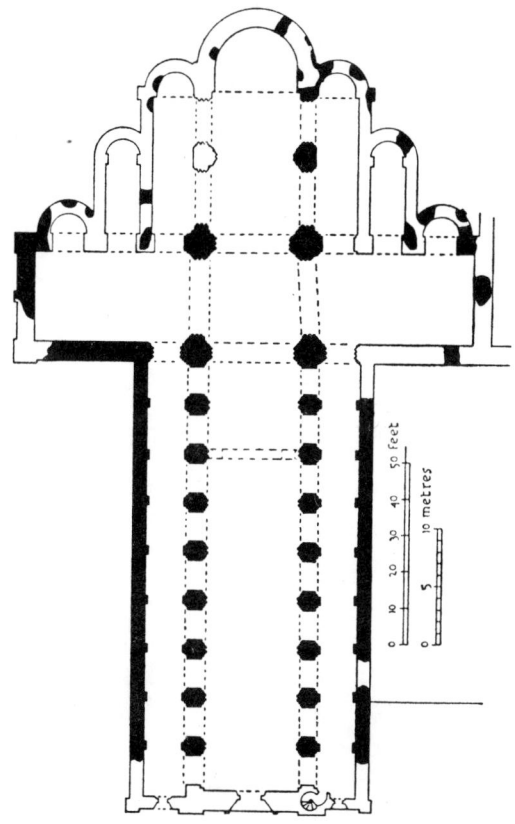

FIG. 8. Binham Priory.

B. THE APSE AND AMBULATORY TYPE.

(1) *Battle* (Fig. 9). Battle Abbey,[1] (Benedictine) founded by the Conqueror on the site of his victory, was colonized by monks from Marmoutier by Tours in 1070 or 1071.[2] The east end of the church was far advanced in 1076[3] and the

---

[1] Dr. Rose Graham, 'The Monastery of Battle' in *Brit. Arch. Ass. Journ.*, N.S., xxx, p. 55.

[2] H. W. C. Davis, *Regesta regum Ang.-Norm.*, i, p. 16.

[3] *Chron. de Bello* (Ang.-Christiana), pp. 9, 26.

Whitby Priory[1] (later Abbey, Benedictine) was refounded by the pilgrim monks from Winchcombe and Evesham, who came to visit the holy places of the north in 1074. The first permanent church, begun towards the close of the century, consisted of a choir of two or three bays with an apse and

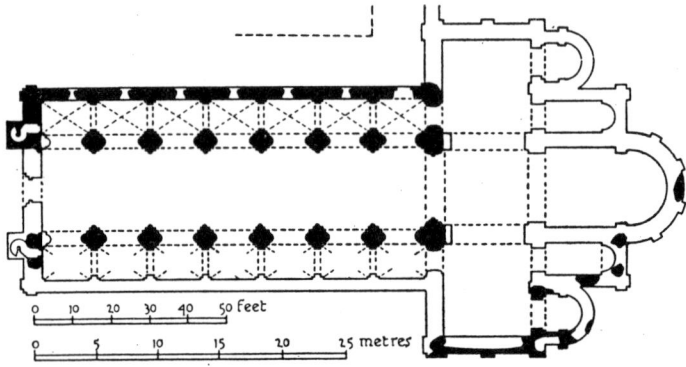

FIG. 7. Blyth Priory.

solid side walls, side-aisles with apses, transepts with apsidal chapels, and an aisled nave. *Blyth Priory*[2] (Notts.) was founded in 1087–8, as a cell of the Benedictine Abbey of the Holy Trinity at Rouen. Its plan (Fig. 7) was similar to that at Whitby but the aisled nave (Pl. 2) of seven bays is still standing largely intact. It is remarkable for its close affinities with the earlier churches of Normandy. *Eye Priory* (Suffolk)[3] was founded about 1075, as a cell of the Benedictine Abbey of Bernay, Normandy. The plan followed very closely (in type and proportions) that of the parent abbey, and differed little in its general lines from those of Whitby, and Blyth, save in its shorter nave of five bays only; the side-apses of the choir had a curved outer face. *Binham Priory*[4] (Norfolk) was perhaps begun just before the close of the eleventh

[1] A. Hamilton Thompson in *Yorks. Arch. Journ.*, xxvii, p. 389.
[2] C. C. Hodges, *Blyth Priory* (1881), and F. H. Fairweather in *Antiq. Journ.*, vi, p. 36.
[3] F. H. Fairweather in *Antiq. Journ.*, vii, p. 299.
[4] F. H. Fairweather in *Ingleby's Sup. to Blomefield's Norfolk*, p. 324, completed by more recent excavations by the same author.

PLATE 2

NORWICH CATHEDRAL, E. END
c. 1096–1100

BLYTH PRIORY, NAVE
c. 1090

whole building was finished in the lifetime of the founder,
who was to have been present at the dedication.[1] This
actually took place in 1094.[2] It is definitely stated that the
monks from Marmoutier superintended the building,[3]
which was of comparatively small dimensions (234 ft. long),
and consisted of a choir of one bay with ambulatory and
three radiating chapels, transepts each with an apsidal

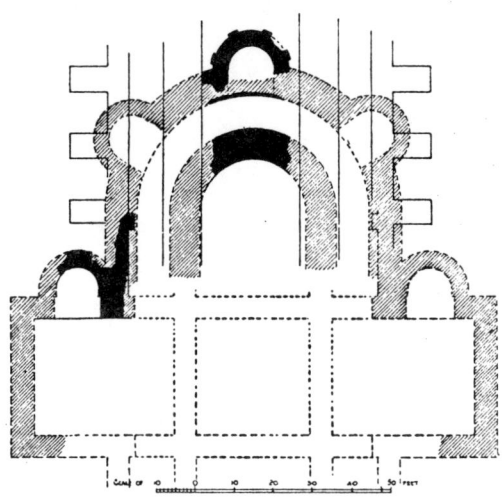

FIG. 9. Battle Abbey.

chapel, and an aisled nave of seven bays. The only part of
the building still standing is the south-west angle of the
nave-aisle with parts of its south wall. Recent excavations[4]
by Sir H. Brakspear have determined the plan of the east
end and transepts.

(2) *Canterbury, St. Augustine's.* St. Augustine's Abbey
church[5] (Benedictine) was begun by Abbot Scotland[6] after
his mission to Rome, between 1070–3. He completed the
eastern arm, transepts, and the first two bays of the nave

[1] *Ibid.*, p. 37. [2] *Ibid.*, pp. 34, 35.
[3] *Ibid.*, p. 23, 'qui operi pre-essent'. [4] *Antiq. Journ.*, xi, p. 166.
[5] *Arch.*, lxvi, p. 377; *Arch. Journ.*, lxxxvi, p. 278.
[6] Gocelin, 'Hist. translat. S. Augustini,' ii, cap. ii, in Migne, *Pat. Lat*, clv, p. 15.
See also *Arch. Journ.* lxiii, p. 107.

before[1] his death in 1087, and the nave was completed by his successor, Wido (1087–99). The church consisted of a choir with ambulatory and three radiating chapels and a crypt (Fig. 23) beneath it, transepts each with an apsidal chapel, and a nave of eleven bays terminating in two western towers in addition. The whole has been excavated within the last twenty-five years and the remains left exposed. The crypt is largely intact except for its arches and vault; but only the lower part of the walls of the superstructure survive, except for a length of the outer wall of the north aisle, and fragments of the west front.

(3) *Bury St. Edmunds* (Benedictine). Bury St. Edmunds Abbey church[2] was begun under Abbot Baldwin[3] (1065–97), who appears to have built only the eastern arm and the crypt under it which were completed when the body of St. Edmund was translated thither in 1095. The nave was probably completed under Abbot Anselm (1119–48), but the west front was finished only under Abbot Sampson[4] (1182–1211). The plan consisted of a choir with ambulatory and three radiating chapels, long transepts of five bays with an eastern aisle and at least one and perhaps two or three apsidal chapels projecting east of it, a nave of twelve bays with a western tower and transept, with flanking chapels. Of this great building the remains are very fragmentary; parts of the central-tower piers, and those adjoining (belonging to the second work), fragments of the north transept with its chapel, various fragments of rubble core, and the ghost of the west front, robbed of all its worked stone, and used as a house.

(4) *Winchester*. The cathedral of Winchester[5] (Bene-

---

[1] The break in the work is distinctly apparent in the foundations.

[2] Dr. M. R. James on the abbey church of St. Edmund at Bury, in *Camb. Antiq. Soc. Comms.*, xxviii, p. 115.

[3] *Memorials of St. Edmund's Abbey* (Rolls Ser.), ii., p. 289.

[4] *Ibid.*, i, p. 291.

[5] R. Willis, 'The architectural history of Winchester Cath.', *Proc. Arch. Inst.*, 1845, p 1; *V.C.H., Hants*, v, p. 50.

PLATE 3

ELY CATHEDRAL, NAVE
early 12th century

PLATE 4

WINCHESTER CATHEDRAL, N. TRANSEPT,
SHOWING GALLERY

c. 1090

dictine) was begun by Bishop Walkelin in 1079.[1] The monks entered the church in 1093,[2] but how much of the nave was then finished is uncertain. The central tower fell in 1107[3] and it and the neighbouring piers were rebuilt shortly afterwards. The church had an apse and ambulatory with an apsidal eastern and square-ended side-chapels, all standing on a crypt (Fig. 21), transepts (Pl. 4) with east and west aisles and galleries across the ends and a nave terminating in a western structure (now mostly destroyed), probably supporting a central western tower. The parts surviving are the crypt, transepts, and the cased and altered walls and piers of the nave. During the building, it was decided to carry up the external angle-bays of both transepts as towers and the supports were strengthened to carry them; they were, however, never completed.

(5) *Worcester*. Worcester Cathedral[4] (Benedictine) was begun by Bishop Wulfstan in 1084[5] and the monks entered the completed choir in 1089.[6] The church was consecrated before 1092[7]. The central tower fell in 1175[8] and the two west bays of the nave were rebuilt, probably after that date. The church consisted of a choir of three bays with apse of seven bays, ambulatory and crypt (Pl. 13), transepts, and a nave of nine bays. Of this there remains the crypt, the two transepts, remains of the start of the triforium, and clearstory of the choir, and some fragments of the nave. The form of the radiating chapels of the choir is uncertain, but some foundations found to the south-east of the ambulatory, led Prof. Willis to suggest that they took the form of square towers; this, however, is very unlikely.

(6) *Old St. Paul's*. The cathedral[9] of St. Paul, London

[1] Rudborne. Ann. Ecc. Wint., Wharton, *Ang. Sac.*, i, p. 294.
[2] *Ibid.*, p. 295. [3] *Ibid.*, p. 297.
[4] R. Willis, 'Architec. Hist. of the Cath. and Monastery of Worcester' in *Arch. Journ.*, xx, p. 83, and H. Brakspear in *V.C.H.*, *Worcester*, iv, p. 394, *The Builder*, Aug. 1892. [5] *Ann. Mon.* (Rolls Ser.), iv, p. 373.
[6] *Heming. Cartul.* (ed. Hearne), p. 419.
[7] *Ibid.*, p. 528. [8] *Ann. Mon.*, iv, p. 383.
[9] Dugdale, *History of St. Paul's Cathedral*.

(secular), was begun by Bishop Maurice[1] probably after the fire which burnt the old cathedral in 1087.[2] Henry of Huntingdon, writing between 1135 and 40, says that it was not then finished. The church consisted of a choir with a crypt below, transepts of five bays with aisles on both sides, and a nave of twelve bays. The form of the east end is not certainly known but William of Malmesbury's remarks on the great extent of the crypt and Wren's opinion[3] that it terminated eastwards in a curve seem to render the apse and ambulatory the most likely plan. Its extent is perhaps indicated by the western limit of the thirteenth-century crypt which terminated four bays east of the crossing. When this was built the curved part of the earlier building was no doubt destroyed and the remainder built up and used as a bone-hole. No remains of the church now survive but the plan and views of the transepts and nave are preserved in Hollar's drawings. Wren thought[4] that the west end of the nave was an extension of uncertain date.

(7) *Gloucester* (Fig. 10). Gloucester Abbey church[5] (Benedictine), now the cathedral, was begun by Abbot Serlo in 1089[6] and consecrated in 1100.[7] At this date probably only the choir and transepts were complete, the nave being certainly of early twelfth-century date. The consecration took place in 1121.[8] The church consisted of a choir of three bays with an apse of three canted sides, ambulatory and three radiating chapels of polygonal form, a crypt (Fig. 22) of the same form, transepts each with an apsidal chapel, a nave (Pl. 5) of eight bays, and two western towers or turrets.[9] Nearly the whole of this structure has survived, though the choir has been recased, the piers of the apse

---

[1] William of Malmesbury, *Gesta Pont.* (Rolls Ser.), p. 145, and Henry of Huntingdon, *Hist. Ang.* (Rolls Ser.), p. 207.
[2] *Two of the Saxon Chronicles Parallel*, ed. Plummer (1892), i, p. 218; ii, p. 217.
[3] Wren, *Parentalia*, p. 272.   [4] *Ibid.*
[5] *V.C.H., Gloucestershire*, ii, p. 53. Plan in *The Builder*, Dec. 1891.
[6] *Hist. et Cart. Glouc.* (Rolls Ser.), i, p. 11.   [7] *Ibid.*, p. 12.
[8] *Florentii Wigorniensis Chron.* (Eng. Hist. Soc.), ii (1849), p. 77.
[9] *Giraldus Cambrensis* (Rolls Ser.), vii, pp. 64–5.

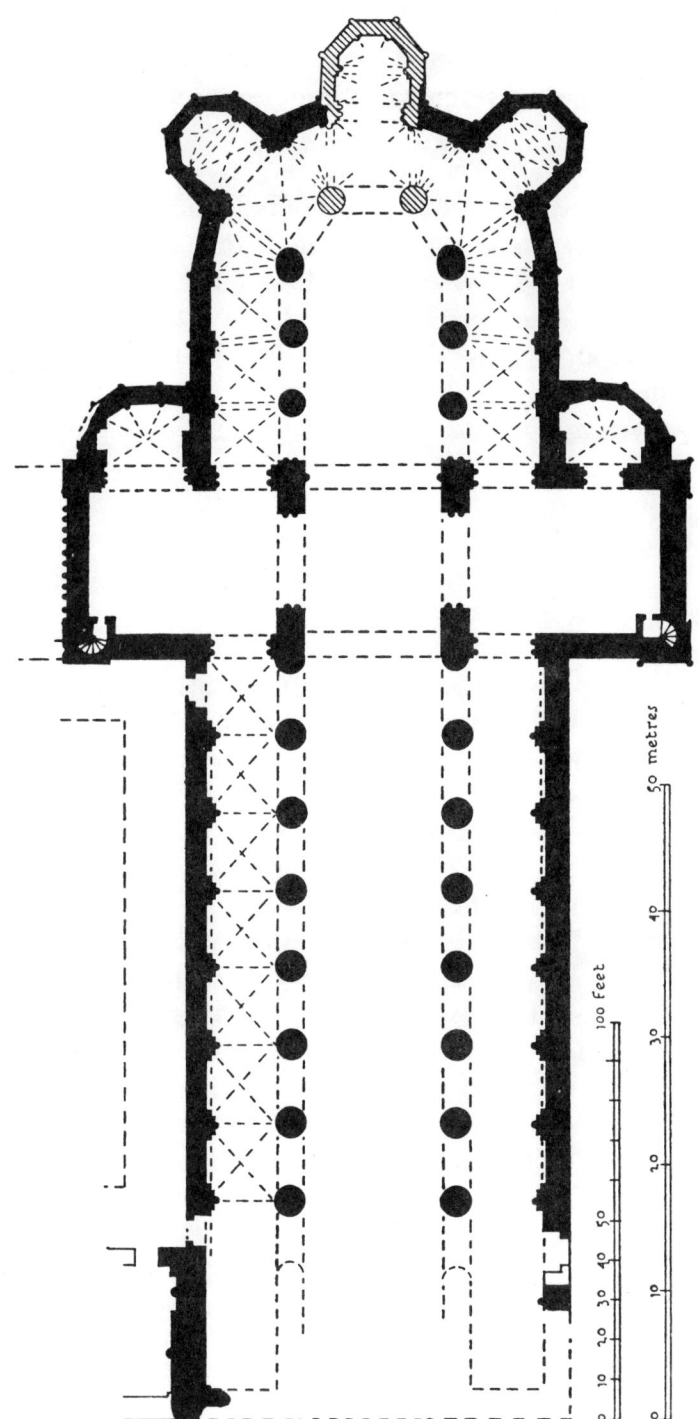

FIG. 10. GLOUCESTER CATHEDRAL.

removed, and the west end of the nave rebuilt, without towers.

(8) *Tewkesbury.* The abbey church of Tewkesbury (Benedictine) was begun by Robert Fitzhamon, after 1087,[1] presumably in preparation for the removal here of the earlier convent at Cranbourne. This removal actually took place in 1102. The church[2] consisted of a choir of two bays with ambulatory and apse of three canted sides like Gloucester, and no doubt three radiating chapels, transepts with eastern apsidal chapels, an aisled nave of eight bays, and a north porch. Practically all this survives intact except for the upper part of the choir, the ambulatory, and the radiating chapels, which were rebuilt in the fourteenth century. The central tower (Pl. 12) was built in the first half of the twelfth century.

(9) *Chichester.* Chichester Cathedral[3] (secular) was begun by Bishop Ralph de Luffa[4] (1091–1123) soon after his accession. It was injured by fire in 1114. Another fire in 1186[5] was more disastrous and led to the extension eastwards, and much other repair by Bishop Seffrid II (1180–1204). This new work was consecrated in 1199.[6] The early church consisted of a choir of three bays with apse and ambulatory, transepts each with an apsidal chapel, and a nave of eight bays including the western towers. The apse and ambulatory were destroyed by the extension of 1186–99, but traces of the spring of the curve remain in the fourth bay of the south aisle. The rest of the building to the west is in great part the original work much altered, and enriched. Traces remain of the north transeptal chapel.

(10) *Chester.* Chester Abbey church[7] (Benedictine), now

---

[1] *Ann. Mon.* (Rolls Ser.), i, p. 44. [2] Plan in *The Builder*, March 1893.
[3] R. Willis, *The Architec. Hist. of Chichester Cathedral.* Plan in *The Builder*, March 1892.
[4] William of Malmesbury, *Gesta Pont.* (Rolls Ser.), p. 206.
[5] Matthew Paris, *Chron. Maj.* (Rolls Ser.), ii, p. 327, and *Gesta Henrici II Benedicti Abbatis* (Rolls Ser.), ii, p. 28.
[6] *Ann. Mon.* (Rolls Ser.), ii (Ann. de Wintonia), p. 73.
[7] Plan in *The Builder*, March 1893.

the cathedral, appears to have been begun about 1092, when the house was refounded as a Benedictine abbey by Hugh, Earl of Chester.[1] The church then begun consisted of a choir of two bays with an apse of five bays, ambulatory, apsidal chapels terminating the side aisles and flanking the main apse, transepts each with an eastern chapel, an aisled nave, now of six bays, and two western towers in addition. Of this there survives much of the north transept, the north wall of the north aisle and the lower part of the north-west tower. The curious planning of the east arm was recovered by excavation[2] about 1845, and the base of one of the main piers is still exposed to view.

(11) *Norwich* (Fig. 11). The cathedral of Norwich[3] (Benedictine) was begun by Bishop Herbert in 1096[4] and finished as far west as the altar of the Holy Cross before his death in 1119.[5] The rest of the building was finished by his successor Everard (1121–45).[6] It consisted of a choir (Pl. 2) of four bays with an apse of five, ambulatory, and three radiating chapels, two of which, were planned on two intersecting segments of circles; transepts each with an apsidal chapel, and a nave of fourteen bays. With the exception of the eastern chapel, and the south transeptal chapel, practically the whole structure survives. It suffered from fire in 1171,[7] when some repairs were made.

In addition to the above a few minor examples of the same type and age must also be mentioned. *St. Martin le Grand* at *Dover*[8] (secular) is not definitely dated, but it seems reasonable to ascribe it to the influence of Ralph Flambard.[9]

[1] William of Malmesbury, *Gesta Pont.* (Rolls Ser.), pp. 78 and 308; *Chetham Soc.*, N.S., 79. Chart. of Chester Abbey, i, pp. xxiii–v.
[2] R. C. Hussey in *Arch. Journ.*, v. p. 17.
[3] H. Harrod, *Castles and Convents of Norfolk* (1857), p. 233; *The Builder*, 1891.
[4] *Chron. Bart. Cotton.* (Rolls Ser.), p. 4.
[5] Reg. Primum of the Cathedral cited in *Norfolk Arch.*, xiv, p. 107.
[6] *Ibid.* The altar of the Holy Cross was four or five bays west of the crossing.
[7] *Chron. Bart. Cotton.*, p. 77.   [8] Plan in *Arch. Cant.*, iv, p. 22.
[9] The church was restored to Flambard by Henry I. *Arch. Aeliana*, 4th ser., vii, pp. 47, 50.

It had a choir of two bays, an apse of five, and an ambulatory with three radiating chapels, transepts, and an aisled nave. The only surviving fragments are parts of the north arcade of the choir, the adjoining aisle, and the north radiating chapel. *Tynemouth Priory*,[1] became in 1085 a cell of St. Albans Abbey and it was probably shortly after this change that the church was begun. It consisted of a choir probably of two bays with an apse, ambulatory, and three radiating chapels, transepts each with an apsidal chapel, and a nave of seven bays. Parts of the crossing, transepts, and nave are still standing.

The foregoing summary of the known particulars of the chief Anglo-Norman churches of the eleventh century will give some indication of the course of development pursued in this country by the buildings of the two types. In considering this the eastern arm must first be dealt with. The earliest English churches of the three-apse type (such as Westminster and Canterbury Cathedral) follow very closely the Norman model, both in their moderate size, and in the two-bay projection of the eastern arm. Almost immediately, however, the choirs of the English churches began to be extended, to three bays at Lincoln and Christchurch, and four at St. Albans, Ely, and Durham. At Lincoln, and perhaps at Ely the main apse was prefaced by a broad arch of slightly narrower span than the main building, while at Durham its place was taken by a complete bay. The side-aisles almost always terminated in apses, and these were commonly finished square externally. The exception at Eye Priory is perhaps due to a conscious copying of the mother-church at Bernay, though a few rather later churches followed the same type. The side walls of the choir at Westminster and St. Albans, probably at Lincoln and possibly at Rochester, were solid, but in the other English examples they seem to have been pierced by open arcades.

[1] W. H. Knowles in *Arch. Journ.*, lxvii, p. 1.

The simplest and probably the earliest of the churches of the ambulatory plan in England was at Battle, where all the dimensions partake of the moderation of the Norman churches. The chief variation in the various east ends of this type is to be found in the form and disposition of the radiating chapels. The traditional French type with three semicircular chapels set radially round the ambulatory is preserved at Battle, St. Augustine's, Canterbury, Tynemouth, St. Martin-le-Grand, Dover, and probably at Bury St. Edmunds. The earliest deviation from this type is found at Winchester, where the east chapel is finished with an apse, and the side chapels are square-ended, and lie on parallel axes to the main church. A variation of this is found at Chester where the side chapels were apsidal but placed on similar axial lines. At Gloucester the three chapels are semi-octagonal, and at Norwich[1] the side pair are formed of two intersecting segments of circles, a form which was later copied at St. Bartholomew, Smithfield.

At Gloucester and Tewkesbury the main apse was supported on only four cylindrical or ovoid piers, and though the superstructure has been, in both cases, destroyed it must have taken the three-sided form, as the interval between the columns is too great for building on the curve. This is one of several features showing the individuality of the school of masons responsible for these and other west-country churches.

Passing now to the other parts of the church, the normal Norman plan of an aisleless transept with a single apsidal chapel in each arm was followed in the majority of the churches of both types detailed above and also at Evesham, Pershore, and elsewhere. As in Normandy these chapels were often of two storys, and the transept itself, as a consequence, provided with a gallery supported on stone

---

[1] The eastern chapel at Norwich, the remains of which were excavated in 1929–30, had a main east apse with a smaller apse for the altar projecting east from it. The remains exhibit work of two periods, *Antiq. Journ.*, xii, p. 117.

vaults and either confined to the projecting portion or extending up to the crossing. Christchurch has definite traces of these extended galleries, which probably existed also at Lincoln, and there is evidence of galleries of the restricted form at Canterbury Cathedral and Ely.[1] The only galleries which survive are those across the transept-ends at Winchester. An elaboration in the plan of the transept is found at St. Albans, Binham, and St. Mary's, York, where there was a pair of apsidal chapels in each arm of differing projection, so that with the three apses of the choir they form an echelon of chapels. This type of transept is widely distributed in France, though St. Ouen, Rouen,[2] is so far the only known early example in Normandy. The transept with east and west aisles first makes its appearance in England at Winchester and the same type was followed at Ely and Old St. Paul's. Yet another variety had only a single aisle, on the east side, first appearing at a single chapel at Lincoln and subsequently as a developed aisle at Durham; at Bury this aisle had an apsidal chapel or chapels to the east of it in each arm.

The naves of the English churches, after the very earliest period, show a very remarkable prolongation extending to 10 bays at St. Albans, 11 at St. Augustine's, Canterbury, 12 at Bury St. Edmunds, and 14 at Norwich.

All these churches had a central tower and, some of them, two western towers in addition. These arrangements are found also in Normandy. The axial western tower found at Ely, Bury, and Winchester is a Saxon inheritance, while the four minor transeptal towers at Winchester must be ascribed to the initiative of the master in charge of the building.

In general, it would appear that the Anglo-Norman builders devoted their energies rather to the dimensions, and particularly the length of their churches than to any

---

[1] Never actually executed in masonry.
[2] The form of the choir here is not definitely known.

definite advance in their structure. Until the building of Durham Cathedral, few of the English churches show any attempt to improve upon or even to emulate the structural system achieved at Caen under William the Conqueror. It is not certain that a stone vault was raised over the main span of any great English church[1] before those at Durham, whereas the ineffective wall-shafts carried up to the roof-plates are almost universally in evidence.

The building of Durham marked a new epoch in the history of Norman Romanesque. Here, as Dr. Bilson has proved, a great Norman church was designed for and eventually erected with a complete system of ribbed vaulting.[2] It may yet be argued whether this great advance was anticipated by a few years in any other French or Italian school, but even if the Norman school only adopted a device which was already known to others, there can be no doubt that the cathedral at Durham shows its application in a form easily eclipsing that of any of its contemporaries. That it originated in the north of England may seem unlikely, but the immediate forbears of the vaults of Durham have all disappeared leaving it in a position of splendid isolation.

Such were the main features of the Anglo-Norman churches of the eleventh century. Their structural details, vaults and crypts will be considered in Chapter III.

Part 2. CHURCHES OF THE FIRST HALF OF THE TWELFTH CENTURY

The first impetus of the Normanization of the English church had hardly exhausted itself by the end of the eleventh century, and the settled reign of Henry I saw a

---

[1] With the probable exception of the choir at Gloucester,
[2] The actual vaulting shows several alterations in execution. The choir was designed for and finished with a complete system of ribbed vaults though the main vault, which was in a dangerous state in 1235, was replaced in the thirteenth century. The north transept was designed for, and retains, its original vault, but that of the south transept is an addition. The main vault of the nave was provided for and built with the triforium and clearstory.

continuation of the building activity of the two preceding reigns. The reconstruction of the few Saxon cathedral and abbey churches, such as Lichfield and Peterborough, which still survived was undertaken. In addition a number of new monastic houses of the first importance were founded, not only of the Benedictine Order but also of the Cluniac Order and of the new Order of Canons Regular.

To this period of activity succeeded one of comparative stagnation. The reign of Stephen (1135–54) was a period of misgovernment, civil strife, and local tyranny which has well deserved its appellation of the Great Anarchy. Here and there the great lords or local magnates might build a church as some make-weight to set against a rapacious career, and Stephen himself founded a monastery at Faversham, but in general church-building on a large scale languished.

This disordered period of twenty years is perhaps some explanation of the little advance made in Anglo-Norman Romanesque after its initial triumphs and after the building of Durham Cathedral had placed it in the forefront of Europe. Such advance as there was, was almost entirely in the elaboration of ornament and not in the improvement of structure; indeed, the accession of Henry II saw English architecture very much at the same point of progress it had reached at the death of Henry I a score of years before.

From one direction only had new life been infused into the art. The advent of the Cistercians and their rapid expansion in England showed how opportune was the arrival of this new ordered and restraining influence in a disordered world. Their activities will be dealt with in a succeeding chapter and the present section will deal only with the general course of Anglo-Norman architecture in the first half of the century, a phase of Romanesque which showed the advance from the severity of the early period to the florid ornament of its middle age.

As we have seen, the larger Anglo-Norman churches of

the eleventh century followed exclusively the two types of plan which we have called the three-apse and the ambulatory plan. These two types persisted side by side during the first quarter of the twelfth century, though examples of the three-apse type become less frequent than those of the ambulatory type. Both began to go out of fashion in the second quarter of the century, and the early twelfth-century churches show a far greater variety in planning than those of the eleventh. Henry I's own foundation (Benedictine) at *Reading*[1] (1121) seems to have had a large church with ambulatory and radiating chapels in the traditional manner, and this plan was followed by the church at *Leominster* (Fig. 12),[2] which became a cell of Reading in 1125. To the same period and type belongs the church of Rahere's priory of Austin Canons at *St. Bartholomew, Smithfield*,[3] founded in 1123; here the radiating chapels followed the curious plan of those at Norwich, formed of two intersecting arcs. The early twelfth-century church of Muchelney Abbey (Benedictine) also followed the apse and ambulatory plan. The post-Conquest cathedral (secular) at Lichfield[4] is not certainly dated but is generally ascribed to the first half of the twelfth century. The foundations of its choir with apse and ambulatory have been found, but nothing else of this age now survives there.

The finest twelfth-century example of the three-apse type is the abbey church (Benedictine) at *Peterborough*[5] (now the cathedral). It was begun by Abbot John de Séez in 1118 and the choir was finished in 1140–3. The rest of the

[1] J. B. Hurry, *Reading Abbey*, 1901. See also *Arch.*, vi, p. 66, and *Berks., Bucks., and Oxon. Arch. Soc. Trans.*, 1880–1, p. 65.

[2] *Arch. Journ.*, x, p. 109. The curious arrangement of the nave-piers at this church would seem to imply the design of carrying a series of heavy cross-arches over the body of the church. The scheme, however, was abandoned before the building of the triforium, and the middle pier was subsequently replaced by an open arch.

[3] *Arch.*, lxiv, p. 165, and *Roy. Com. on Hist. Mons., London*, iv, p. 123.

[4] Prof. Willis in *Arch. Journ.*, xviii, p. 1, with plan.

[5] C. R. Peers in *V.C.H., Northants*, ii, p. 431.

building followed in due course, the nave being finished by Abbot Benedict (1177–94) who prolonged it by two bays.

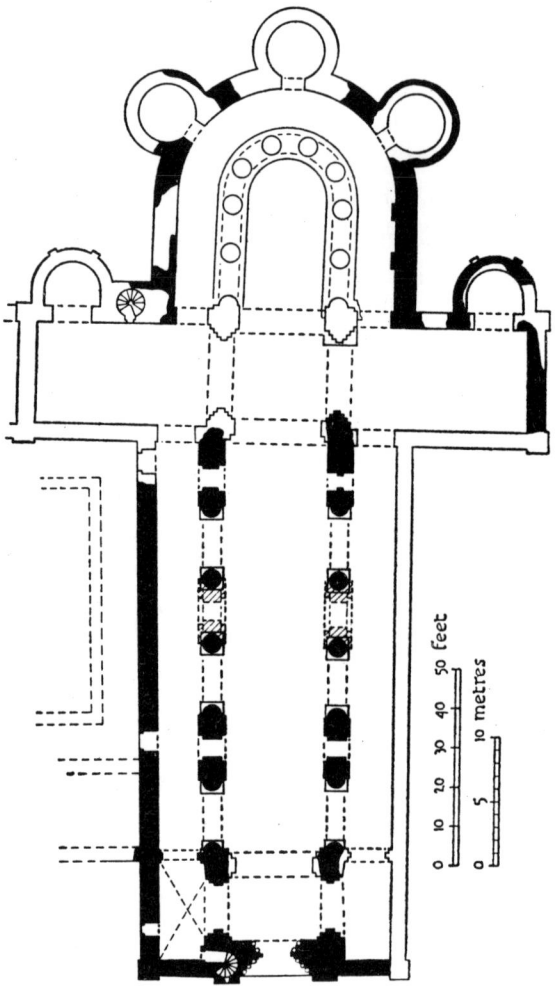

FIG. 12. Leominster Priory.

Selby Abbey[1] (Benedictine) though founded as early as 1069, was transferred to the present site[2] by the second

[1] Architectural account by C. C. Hodges in *Coucher Book of Selby* (Yorks. Arch. Soc. Record Ser.), i, Introduction.

[2] *Coucher Book of Selby*, i, p. 22.

abbot, Hugh de Lacy (1097–1111). The church, begun probably early in the twelfth century, consisted of an apsidal choir of two bays, side-aisles with apses, transept with an apsidal chapel in each arm, and a nave of seven bays with western towers in addition. The north transept, crossing, and nave only survive, the south transept having been mostly destroyed and the choir replaced by a fourteenth-century structure. The plan of the first east end has been partly recovered by excavation. The nave shows several distinct campaigns of construction extending to the latter part of the twelfth century and beyond.

Wymondham Priory,[1] a cell to St. Albans, was founded in 1107. The side-apses of the choir were semicircular both inside and out. The nave (of twelve bays including the destroyed pair of west towers) is still standing. A fourth example has been excavated at the Benedictine nunnery at Shaftesbury,[2] and Barking,[3] another great nunnery of the same order, probably had the same type of plan.

An early modification of the three-apse type of plan consisted of the squaring of the main east end of the choir, while retaining the side-apses of the earlier form. Such were the churches of *Southwell*[4] (secular), and *St. Martin's* (new work), *Dover*,[5] a cell of Canterbury Cathedral. The former (Fig. 13) was begun by Archbishop Thomas (1108–14), and though the original choir has been destroyed, the transepts, nave of seven bays, central and two western towers remain. The church at Dover was built by Archbishop Corbeuil in 1131. Its plan has been recovered by excavation, but nothing but a few shapeless fragments of the west end now remain.

---

[1] F. H. Fairweather in *Ingleby's Sup. to Blomefield's Norfolk*, p. 328.
[2] E. Doran Webb, *Reports on the Excavations*, 1904. The foundations have again been uncovered recently.
[3] *Essex Arch. Soc. Trans.*, xii, p. 69.
[4] A. Hamilton Thompson in *Thoroton Soc. Trans.*, xv, p. 15; G. M. Livett, *Southwell Minster*, 1883; T. H. Clarke, *Southwell Collegiate Church*, 1838. Plan in *The Builder*, July 1892. Plans of east end in *Ass. Archit. Socs. Reports*, xx, p. 55.
[5] *Arch. Cant.*, iv, p. 1.

A variant of the ambulatory plan, which makes its appearance in the same period, may almost be regarded

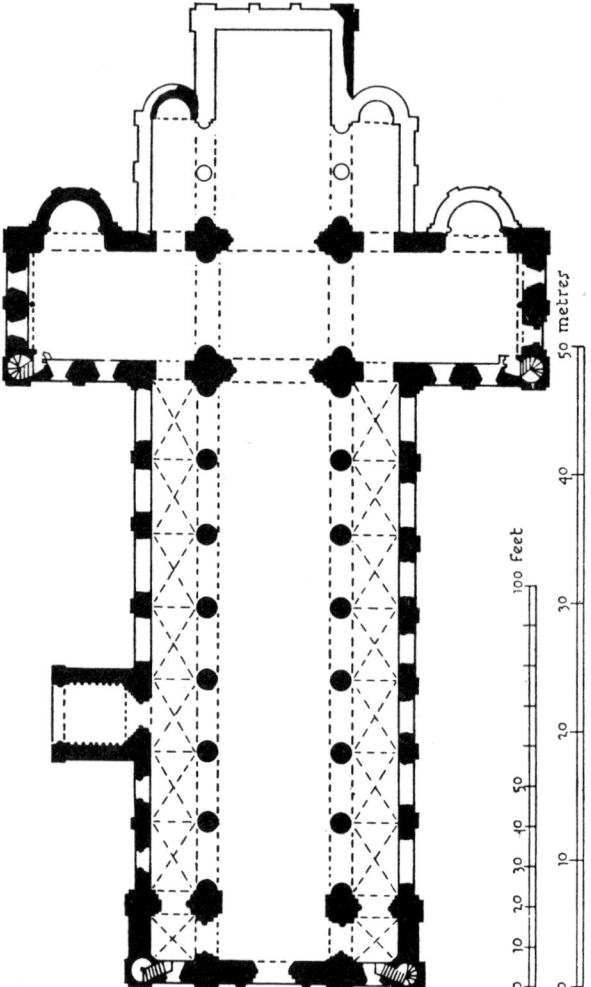

FIG. 13. Southwell Minster.

as a new type. It consisted of a square-ended choir with an ambulatory carried round it and a chapel or chapels projecting to the east of the ambulatory. The scheme was treated in a variety of ways and no two examples are quite the same; it will consequently be best to tabulate the chief examples.

(1) *Chertsey* (Fig. 14). The excavations of 1861 on the site of Chertsey Abbey[1] (Benedictine) showed that the choir here had a single arch in the square east end and three apsidal chapels projecting from the ambulatory beyond it. An entry in the *Anglo-Saxon Chronicle* under the year 1110[2] gives definite evidence for the beginning of this church, but unfortunately nothing except the base of the south wall of the choir-aisle is now visible.

(2) *Romsey*. The Benedictine nuns' church at Romsey[3] was probably begun about 1120, and proceeded slowly westwards, the nave not being finished until the thirteenth century. The eastern arm (Pl. 7) consisted of a choir of three bays with two arches in the east wall, apsidal chapels at the ends of the aisles and a chapel of uncertain form between them, entered from the ambulatory by two arches. The rest of the plan is normal. The church survives intact except for the east chapel.

(3) *Old Sarum*. The eastern parts of the cathedral (Fig. 4) were rebuilt[4] and extended by Bishop Roger (1103–39) probably *c.* 1125–30. The footings of this extension were excavated in 1912 and showed that it consisted of a square-ended choir of four bays with aisles and ambulatory and three chapels projecting to the east of it; these chapels were square-ended externally but may have been apsidal within. At the same time the transepts were rebuilt with aisles on both sides.

(4) *Rochester*. We have seen that the square east end at Rochester, of which the foundations have been discovered, can hardly have to do with Gundulf's cathedral. The western part of the crypt, with which this east end appears to be contemporary, is of early type, and may well have

---

[1] S. Angel. *The Excavations on the site of Chertsey Abbey 1861*.

[2] *Anglo-Saxon Chron.* (Rolls Ser.), i, p. 369.

[3] *V.C.H., Hants*, iv, p. 460.

[4] *Proc. Soc. Ants.*, xxvi, p. 100.

formed part of an extension by Bishop Ernulf (1115–25). As shown on Sir Wm. Hope's plans,[1] with the main arcades continued to the east wall, it belongs to a type unknown at this period. If, on the contrary, the choir was finished square a bay to the west of the foundations discovered, the east bay forming an ambulatory, it falls naturally into place in the series we are now considering.

A curious arrangement, which may indicate a similar plan with later modifications, is preserved in a sixteenth-century plan[2] of the Augustinian priory of *Holy Trinity, Aldgate* (London), founded *c.* 1108. The extreme central part of the eastern arm, with its semi-octagonal apse, would appear to be a later extension.

A second new type is exemplified by a west-country group which includes *Hereford Cathedral, St. John's* at *Chester,* and perhaps *Llandaff Cathedral* (all secular). This type was a modification of the three-apse plan; it had a square east end from which projected three apses of no great height. The arch opening into the main apse itself was of no greater height than the main arcades of the building. *Hereford* (Fig. 15)[3] has a choir of three bays and had a pair of towers rising over the east bays of the choir aisles; both towers and apses have now been destroyed. This church was begun by Bishop Reynelm (1107–15) but was not completed till some fifty years later. The eastern arm of *St. John's* at *Chester*[4] is much ruined, but was formerly of four or five bays. The western bay is incorporated in the present church and the arches opening into the main and north side apses still remain. The church does not seem to have been begun much before 1130–40. The remains of the twelfth-century cathedral at *Llandaff*[5] (begun in 1120) are of less completeness; the main east arch and portions of the side walls of the choir still survive.

---

[1] *Arch. Cant.,* xxiii, p. 242. [2] *Home Counties Mag.,* ii, p. 46.

[3] *Roy. Com. on Hist. Mons., Hereford,* i, p. 93.

[4] *Chester Archit. Arch. and Hist. Soc.,* ii, p. 329.

[5] E. W. Lovegrove in *Brit. Arch. Assoc. Trans.,* N.S., xxxv, p. 75.

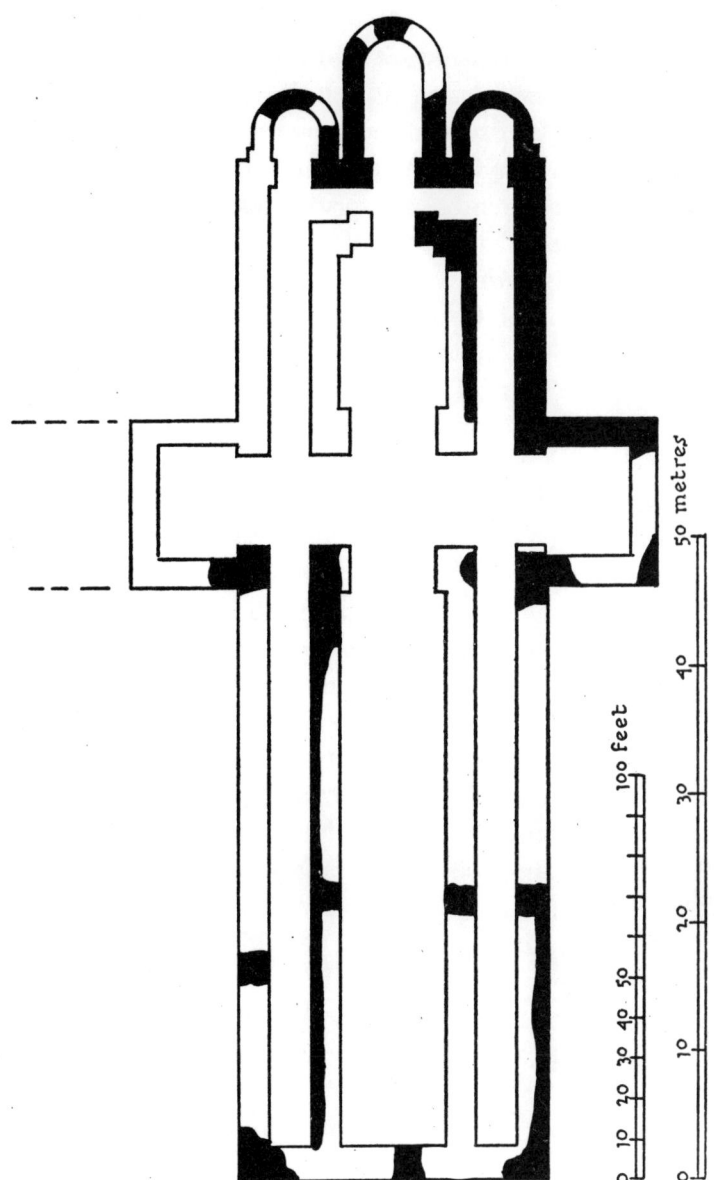

FIG. 14. Chertsey Abbey.

The cathedral of *Exeter*[1] (secular) is said to have been begun by Bishop Warelwast in 1117 and not to have been finished[2] until the time of Bishop Marshall (1194–1206). It stood in a class by itself not only by reason of the two towers over the transepts, which still exist, but also because the choir of two or three bays appears to have terminated in a polygonal apse. The record of the discovery of this feature is not very satisfactory, and it is just possible that this apse was a fragment of Canute's minster of 1019. Transeptal towers similar to those at Exeter may, as we have seen, have formed part of the eleventh-century cathedral at Sarum, but the ultimate origin of the type remains obscure.

The greater number of the major eleventh-century churches were planned on so large a scale that no extension was found necessary until a much later date. A few, however, built on purely Norman lines and scale, immediately after the Conquest, were soon found to be insufficient in extent for the more ambitious views of a later generation. Some of these have already been dealt with, but the most important instance, *Canterbury Cathedral*,[3] remains to be described. The extension (Fig. 16) at Canterbury, begun by Prior Ernulf (1096–1107) and completed by Prior Conrad (1108–1126) consisted of a crypt and an aisled presbytery of nine bays with an apse and ambulatory of seven bays; it had eastern transepts each with two apsidal chapels and three rectangular radiating chapels of which the western pair had apses towards the east. With the exception of the main arcades much of this work was incorporated in the rebuilding and further extension of the church after the fire of 1174.

[1] H. E. Bishop and E. K. Prideaux, *The Building of the Cathedral Church of Exeter*, 1922; also W. R. Lethaby in *Archit. Review*, xiii (1903), pp. 109 and 166; and *Exeter Dio. Arch. Soc.*, N.S., v, p. 120. Plan also in *The Builder*, June 1891.

[2] The new church was entered by the canons in 1133, as recorded in the Annals of Tavistock Abbey, Bodleian MS. Digby 81, fo. 88. This no doubt dates the completion of the choir. F. Rose Troup, *The Consecration of the Norman Minster at Exeter*, 1933.

[3] R. Willis, *Architectural History of Canterbury Cathedral*.

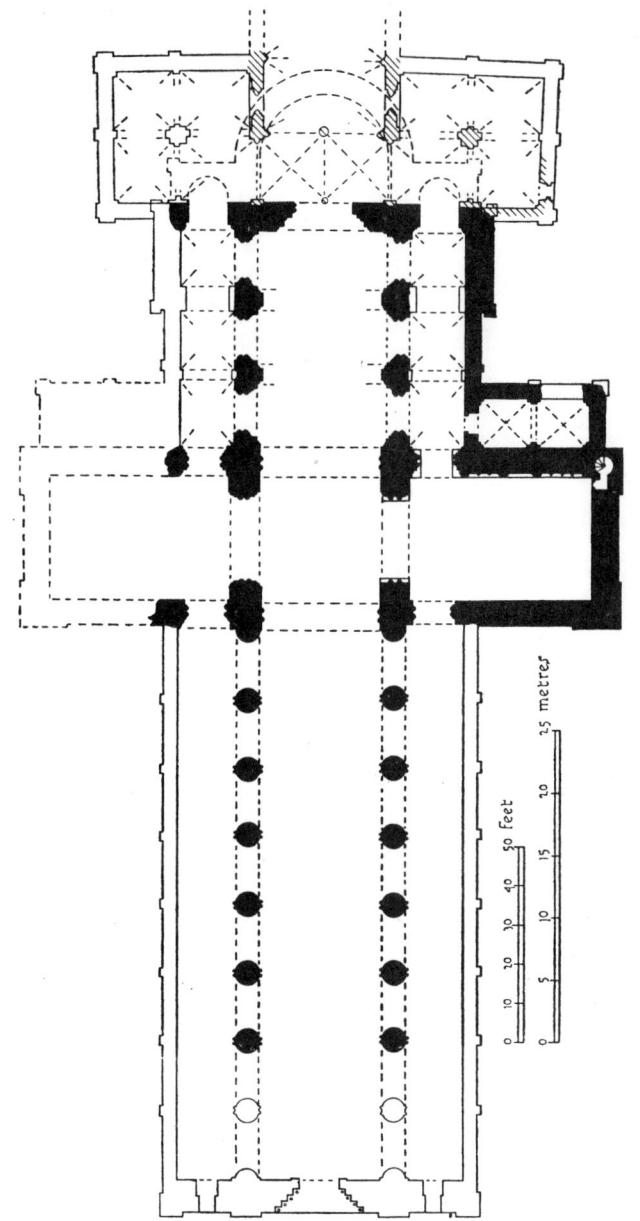

FIG. 15. HEREFORD CATHEDRAL.

To a certain extent these new types were, no doubt, influenced by the architectural models affected by some of the newer religious orders, the enlargement at Canterbury being probably inspired by the plan of the great church at Cluny. These external influences will be dealt with in a subsequent chapter.

Chapter III

COMPONENT PARTS OF LATE ELEVENTH-
AND EARLY TWELFTH-CENTURY CHURCHES

IN the two parts of the last chapter we have passed in
review the general form and types of plan used in the
Anglo-Norman churches down to about the middle of
the twelfth century. In the first period the severity of the
Norman prototype was largely retained, and it was not
until the twelfth century that this gave place to the greater
variety and more lavish decoration which marked the
second period of Anglo-Norman Romanesque.

Our survey of the structure of the churches of these two
periods must now be completed by an examination of the
component parts of the superstructure and substructure
which do not enter essentially into the composition of the
plan.

(a) *Piers.* The piers of the main arcades of the Anglo-
Norman churches are of three types—square, cylindrical, or
compound. Square or rectangular piers are the simplest
form and are only very occasionally employed in the larger
churches. The angles are generally broken by one or more
recesses or rebates continuing the orders of the arches above.
The type in its plainest form can be seen in the nave of
Chepstow Priory, and with very little elaboration in the
nave of St. Albans Abbey, but at St. Albans the simple
form is almost necessitated by the use of Roman brick as
the staple building material.

The cylindrical pier is used either alone or in alternation
with the compound form. As used alone it forms the distinguishing feature in a remarkable group of churches in
the west country, of which Evesham Abbey[1] nave may
perhaps have been the prototype. This church, now

[1] Plan of Excavations in *Vetusta Monumenta*, v, Pl. lxvii.

destroyed except for the foundations, was completed as far west as the nave[1] during the Conqueror's reign; the nave, begun in the same period, as is indicated[2] by a statement in the Chronicle and by surviving mouldings, had cylindrical piers, of heavy type, though it is now impossible to say what was their relative height. The surviving examples are

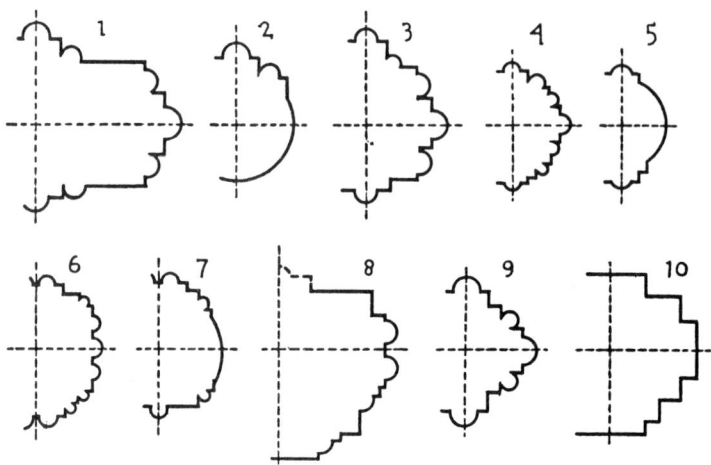

FIG. 17. Comparative Plans of Piers.

1. Durham Choir. Major pier. 2. Durham Choir. Minor pier. 3. Winchester Transept. W. aisle. 4. Ely Nave. Major pier. 5. Ely Nave. Minor pier. 6. Norwich Nave. Major pier. 7. Norwich Nave. Minor pier. 8. Hereford Choir. 9. Romsey Nave. 10. St. Alban's Nave.

the naves of Gloucester (c. 1120), Tewkesbury (c. 1120–30), and remains of the nave at Pershore (c. 1120); the piers (Pl. 5) in this group are differentiated by their great size and massiveness—they average about 6 ft. in diameter—and still more by their extreme height (Gloucester 30½ ft., Tewkesbury 30¾ ft., Pershore 25 ft.). This last feature has the effect of entirely dwarfing the triforium and clearstory, which are indeed reduced far below their normal vertical dimensions. It is difficult to suggest a reasonable theory of the origin of this type, which is quite unknown in Normandy.[3] Elsewhere

[1] *Chron. Abb. Evesham* (Rolls Ser.), p. 55.   [2] *Ibid.*, p. 98.
[3] Dr. Bilson considers that at Gloucester and Tewkesbury the choir had an intermediate triforium-story between the main triforium or tribune and the

in France the use of the tall cylindrical pier, as at Tounurs, S. Savin, and elsewhere, is not unknown, but is found in a connexion totally dissimilar from that which obtains at Gloucester, and one is forced to the conclusion that the Gloucester masters were alone responsible for the production of a type which is more striking than admirable. The use of the cylindrical pier of normal proportions is fairly common in other parts of England. Well-proportioned arcades of this

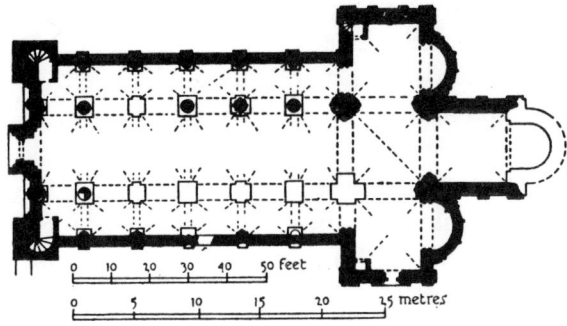

FIG. 18. Lindisfarne Priory.

type survive at Hereford Cathedral, Carlisle Cathedral, and elsewhere, and a more squat variety in the naves of Southwell Cathedral, Great Malvern Priory, and St. John's at Chester. The same form of pier was commonly used also for the arcade of the main apse in an ambulatory plan.[1]

The cylindrical pier, used in alternation with the compound pier, is a fashion derived directly from Jumièges Abbey; it first appears definitely[2] in England at Durham, (Frontispiece) to be followed at Waltham Holy Cross[3] and Lindisfarne Priory (Fig. 18).[4] The purpose in all these

clearstory. The proportions of the nave were arrived at by suppressing entirely the main triforium and making the main arcade the height of the two lower storys, while retaining the levels of the minor triforium and clearstory.

[1] E.g. Winchester Cathedral (destroyed), St. Bartholomew Smithfield, Tewkesbury, Chester Cathedral (destroyed), and Gloucester. At Norwich, however, the apse has a series of compound piers.

[2] The foundations of the nave of the Confessor's church at Westminster probably indicate the same arrangement though only the square plinths of the intermediate piers survive.

[3] *Roy. Com. on Hist. Mons., Essex*, ii, p. 238.   [4] *The Builder*, June 1895.

examples was the production of a double bay, though this hardly ever produced the square plan required for the corresponding vault over the main body of the building. The same arrangement was originally designed in the eastern part of Norwich Cathedral nave.[1]

The simplest form of compound pier is that consisting of a square with half-round shafts set against each face. Piers of this type were not common in Normandy, and in England also they were but little used, their place being taken by the later elaborated form, also employed in Normandy. This form has additional shafts either recessed or applied, such as may be seen at Winchester, Ely, Peterborough, and numerous other churches. Occasionally an attempt has been made at the combination of the compound and cylindrical pier, in which the cylindrical form emerges as a curved surface from one or more faces. A certain purely decorative alternation is observable in some buildings where the compound pier prevails; thus in the nave at Ely every alternate pier has a flat semi-cylindrical shaft supporting the two inner orders of the main arches instead of the single round shaft to each order of the other piers.

(b) *Triforium* and *Clearstory*. The triforium stage is sometimes lit only from the interior of the church by the openings above the main arcades; more usually, however, there seems to have been a single small window in the outer wall of each bay. These can still be seen at Norwich, Chichester, Christchurch, Gloucester, and elsewhere. The openings on the inner side are sometimes plain and round-headed as in St. Albans nave, but more commonly are divided up by two sub-arches springing from shafts, and having a solid tympanum above as at Winchester, Durham, Hereford, Ely, Peterborough, and Christchurch Priory. A later development (Pl. 7), exemplified at Romsey Abbey (Hants), consists in making the sub-arches free, and inserting a little shaft with capital and base under the crown

[1] *Norfolk Archaeology*, xiv, p. 105.

PLATE 5

GLOUCESTER CATHEDRAL, N. AISLE OF NAVE
c. 1120 and later

DURHAM CATHEDRAL, NAVE
finished c. 1130

PLATE 6

DURHAM CATHEDRAL, N. TRANSEPT, E. CLEARSTORY
AND VAULT

c. 1104–10

DURHAM CATHEDRAL, N. TRANSEPT, E. TRIFORIUM

c. 1100

PLATE 7

NORTHAMPTON, ST. PETER, NAVE
c. 1160–70

ROMSEY ABBEY, N. SIDE OF CHOIR
c. 1120–30

PLATE 8

GLOUCESTER CATHEDRAL, TRIFORIUM OF CHOIR
c. 1095

NORWICH CATHEDRAL, LANTERN OF CENTRAL TOWER
c. 1110

of the main arch. In the twelfth century the sub-arches were sometimes increased in number, as at St. Bartholomew Smithfield. Another form of triforium-opening consists of a series of open arches of the same span and not unlike the main arcade below but of less height. This form may be seen at Southwell,[1] Norwich, and Thorney Abbey.

The actual triforium story, extending over the aisle below, was generally covered by the sloping timber roof over the aisle vaults. At Gloucester (choir), however, it received a half barrel-vault (Pl. 8), as an abutment for the main vault of the choir. The triforium at St. John's chapel in the Tower of London has a complete barrel-vault.[2]

The clearstory, in its simplest form, had a single round-headed window in each bay. More commonly, however, this window was flanked by a pair of lower arches, behind which and in front of the window ran the clearstory passage. Southwell is remarkable in having a round window in each bay with a barrel-vaulted passage between it and the round-headed arch opening into the nave.

(c) *Vaults*.[3] The whole system of the late eleventh-century churches of Normandy and England, as we have already indicated, has been thought to imply the ultimate aim of achieving a clearstoried building completely covered by stone vaults. In the vast majority of cases the piers are provided with shafts, not only towards the aisles, but also towards the main body of the building; these shafts should, logically, be a provision for the support either of a high

[1] There is evidence of an intention to subdivide the triforium at Southwell, and the blocks left at the crowns of the arches suggest the use of small supporting shafts like those at Romsey.

[2] A curious and perhaps unique (in England) arrangement of the triforium is to be seen in the nave at Rochester (Pl. 22). Here, probably after the fire of 1137, the vault of the aisle was removed and a triforium passage contrived in the thickness of the main wall, between the triforium openings, the aisle being covered by a pent-roof above the triforium arches.

[3] John Bilson, 'The Norman School, and the Beginnings of Gothic Architecture', in *Arch. Journ.*, lxxiv, p. 1; 'Durham Cathedral. The Chronology of its Vaults', *ibid.*, lxxix, p. 101.

vault or of diaphragm-arches; the vault of the triforium at Gloucester,[1] as well as the abutting arches found in the triforia of Chichester and Norwich, are meaningless, unless they imply at least the intention to roof the main span in stone, for the alternative diaphragm-arch seems not to have been employed in England. That, when it came to the point, the intention was often abandoned is an indication only of lack of confidence, or lack of funds. In the earliest Norman and Anglo-Norman churches the aisles and apses only were vaulted, the latter generally with semi-domes, and the former with a series of plain groined vaults over the bays, divided by plain cross-arches. These groined vaults were built on a semi-cylindrical centering, with cross-centering built up on it; they are constructed of rubble with some rough cutting of the stones forming the groins. The cross-arches are semicircular and the groins follow a roughly elliptical curve which had a common tendency to sag in the middle. To obviate this certain vaults in the crypts of Winchester and Gloucester are formed with slightly sloping crowns up to the middle of the vault. Occasionally in Normandy, as we have seen, the main spans were also covered by groined vaults, and examples of these still survive over the choirs of S. Nicolas and the Trinité at Caen. In England, remains of only one such vault actually exist, in the nave of Chepstow Priory (Fig. 19),[2] founded as a cell of Cormeilles Abbey before 1071,[3] and of which the nave may be assigned to c. 1120. Here very broad cross-arches divided the bays, with a groined vault between them. The vault itself has been destroyed, but sufficient remains, against the side walls, to indicate the arrangement.

[1] There was, almost certainly, a stone vault over the choir of Gloucester, as there is definite evidence of a twelfth-century vault over the nave of the same church. There are, furthermore, traces of an intention to vault the nave of Peterborough, a scheme abandoned before the completion of the clearstory.

[2] C. Lynam, 'The Nave of Chepstow Church', in *Arch. Journ.*, lxii, p. 270.

[3] R. Graham, 'Four Alien Priories of Monmouthshire', in *Brit. Arch. Assoc. Journ.*, N.S., xxxv, p. 103.

Precisely the same system was also adopted in two Essex
village churches, Copford (Fig. 33 b) and Great Clacton,
but here again the vaults have been removed.

The next step in the development of the vault was the
reinforcing of the weak point, the groins, by cut stone ribs
on which the rubble of the vault itself rested. The earliest
and most obvious form consisted of the two diagonal ribs

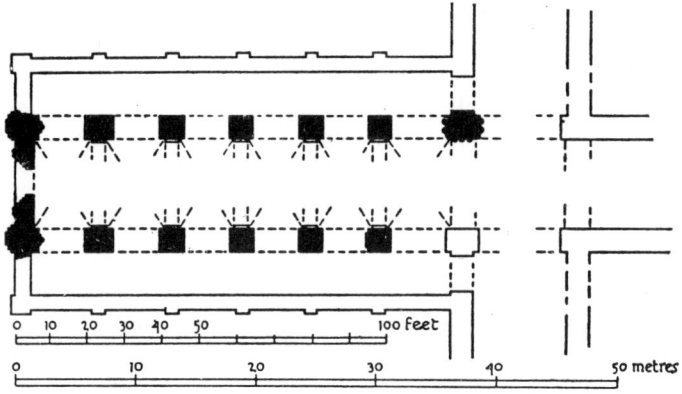

FIG. 19. Chepstow Priory.

only, crossing at the crown of the vault, and forming four
cells or spandrels in each bay.

The origin of this quadripartite ribbed vault is of the
utmost importance for the study of architectural development, as it was the first step taken towards the constructional
system of Gothic. Much has been written on the subject,
and attempts have been made to establish its chronological
priority in various provinces of France and Italy. Since the
publication of the detailed analysis of the vaults of Durham
by Dr. John Bilson, however, there can be little doubt of the
priority of this example over any important surviving com-
petitor in France by fifteen years or more.

The earlier forms of the ribbed vault show their immediate descent from the groined vault by the ribs which
cover the groins following as far as possible the depressed
curve of the earlier unribbed groin. Very soon, however,

this somewhat awkward arrangement was got rid of by making the diagonal ribs semicircular and stilting the cross-arches to raise them to the same height. At Durham the vaults of the choir-aisles were built by 1096, the original main vault of the choir by 1104, that over the north transept by *c.* 1110, and the others over the south transept and nave by about 1130. Of these vaults those over the choir-aisles show the earlier peculiarities mentioned above. In addition to the Durham vaults, the ribbed vaults in the transept-aisles at Winchester were built after the fall of the tower in 1107, and those in the choir-aisles at Peterborough soon after the beginning of that work in 1118. All these examples are earlier than any dated examples in France, and though the Durham vaults are too mature to be an initial attempt, they appear to be the earliest which have survived.

The next development of the ribbed vault was the production of the sexpartite form. This is adapted for vaulting a double bay, the additional rib, producing the six cells, being sprung from the intermediate wall-shaft dividing the subsidiary bays. Side by side with this form appears the quasi-sexpartite vault, which is really a quadripartite vault with the additional rib supporting a diaphragm-wall under the crown of each bay. Examples of the two forms may be seen in the naves of S. Étienne (*c.* 1130), and the Trinité (rather later and now rebuilt) at Caen, but the sexpartite form does not occur in England until a much later date, and the quasi-sexpartite vault not at all. A final development of the Norman school of vaulting is the octopartite[1] vault to be found over the lantern stage of the tower at Montivilliers (*c.* 1140) and the similar vault over the Treasury at Canterbury (*c.* 1150). In both these instances the ribs spring from the same level and meet at the crown; the vault-cells slope steeply downwards, and are arched over the window-heads at Montivilliers and stopped over wall-arches at Canterbury.

[1] John Bilson. *Arch. Journ.*, lxxiv, p. 1.

PLATE 9

ST. ALBANS CATHEDRAL, CROSSING AND LANTERN
c. 1080–90

PLATE 10

EXETER CATHEDRAL, S. TOWER
c. 1140

BURY ST. EDMUNDS ABBEY,
GATE TOWER
c. 1130

Turning now to the second form of early vaulting—the barrel-vault—we find its use as infrequent in England as it was in Normandy. The only definite example of its use over a wide span is in St. John's chapel (Pl. 11) in the Tower of London (c. 1080), where it is finished continuously with a semi-dome over the apse and is found in conjunction with groined vaults over the aisles and barrel-vaults over the triforium. As the chapel is contained in the structure of the keep, there was here no possibility of clearstory lighting, and consequently no advantage in the groined form.

Barrel-vaults appear also in a number of smaller buildings such as the Dark Cloister at Westminster, the corresponding building at Norwich, the porch at Southwell, the village church of Kempley (Glos.), the crypts at Christchurch[1] (Hants) and Chilton Candover (Hants), and, at a much later date, over the chapter-house at Gloucester. The last example has transverse ribs at intervals under the soffit as have the outer parlour at Norwich and an apartment in the Deanery at Gloucester.

(d) *Towers*. The vast majority of eleventh- and early twelfth-century Norman churches above the rank of parish church were provided with a central tower. Subsidiary towers were placed either centrally over the west front in the Anglo-Saxon tradition, or over the west bays of the nave-aisles in the Norman tradition. Occasionally they were placed beyond the aisles[2] to enlarge the spread of the west front.

A large number of Anglo-Norman central towers collapsed either soon after their erection, as at Winchester in 1107, or at a later date, like those at Worcester in 1175, Evesham about 1207, Bury St. Edmunds in 1210, Lincoln in 1240, and Ely in 1322. The earliest towers of this class were built with equal arches on all the four sides, but

[1] The apses of the two transeptal crypts have ribbed vaults of early form dating from c. 1110.

[2] E.g. St. Botolph's Priory, Colchester, and, as I am informed by Dr. Fairweather, Earl's Colne Priory, Essex.

owing to a recognition of this insecurity due to bad foundations, and sometimes to faulty structure, it became the custom in the twelfth century or even earlier to reduce the span of the transept arches by deep responds while retaining the full width towards the chancel and nave.[1] Even this was not wholly successful, for the twelfth-century crossing-arches of St. Bartholomew Smithfield, Hereford, and elsewhere had subsequently to be reinforced to support their own weight or that of a heightened superstructure. These central towers were commonly, in the distinctively Norman fashion, open to the crossing, forming a lantern, and were enriched with one or more internal arcades and wall-passages (Pl. 8).

The central tower at St. Albans is perhaps the only one belonging to the greater eleventh-century churches which now survives. It is built of Roman brick, rises two external stages above the roofs, and has an internal gallery and lantern. The four supporting arches (Pl. 9) are the full width of the crossing, and the round arches are plastered and painted to represent alternate voussoirs of white and yellow stone.

The most important surviving central towers of the second period are those at Norwich (Pl. 8), Tewkesbury (Pl. 12), and Southwell. All three have external ranges of intersecting arcading, and Norwich has an unusual double range of sound-holes[2] to the belfry. Norwich also retains most of its original angle-turrets.

The pairs of western towers survive complete at Durham, Southwell, and Worksop Priory. In each case they form the natural terminations of the nave-aisles and are not set beyond them. The two former are enriched with arcading, but at Worksop, though of the end of the twelfth century, the architecture is severely plain. At Lincoln also the

---

[1] E.g. Gloucester, Chichester, St. Bartholomew Smithfield, Hereford, Malmesbury, &c.
[2] The lower range is blind.

eleventh- and twelfth-century western towers survive, but they have been greatly heightened in the fifteenth century.

Axial towers, one over the crossing and one over the west end of the nave, have in no instance both survived. At Ely the west tower is standing but the central tower has been destroyed. The west tower at Leominster, though of the twelfth century, is an addition to the original design, and here again the central tower has been destroyed. At Winchester the twelfth-century central tower survives, but the west tower was destroyed in the fourteenth century.[1] At Malling Abbey[2] (Kent) the west tower is an addition to the original structure of Bishop Gundulf. The upper stage is octagonal with turrets at the angles of the square stage below.

Towers over the transepts were an unusual feature in this country, but an instance occurs at Exeter (Pl. 10) where both towers are still standing; they date from the first half of the twelfth-century, and have an elaborate arcaded enrichment. It is possible that these towers were copied from an earlier example at the cathedral of Old Sarum, begun by Bishop Hermann about 1075. Here only the ground-plan remains, but this seems to indicate the absence of a central tower and the presence of towers over the transepts. The Exeter transeptal towers were copied late in the thirteenth century at Ottery St. Mary.

A still more unusual arrangement is that of which evidence survives at the cathedral at Hereford. Here there were towers over the east bays of the choir-aisles as well as one over the crossing. These eastern towers would seem to be a borrowing from German Romanesque and more particularly from the Rhine valley, where towers in this or a similar position are not uncommon. At Hereford both towers were removed in the thirteenth century.

We have noted also the intention to raise subsidiary

---

[1] Petersfield church (Hants) had a twelfth-century central tower, and a rather later west tower still survives.   [2] *Arch. Journ.*, lxxxviii, p. 175.

towers over the ends of the transept-aisles at Winchester. This was a very early break-away from the pure Norman tradition, and, though not accomplished, shows the early inventiveness of the Anglo-Norman master-mason.

Round towers in England are confined to parish churches and are to be found most frequently in the counties of Norfolk, Suffolk, Essex, and Sussex.[1] In East Anglia there are a few—Professor Baldwin Brown[2] gives two only— which may be assigned to the late pre-Conquest period, while a number more belong to the immediately succeeding age. Their occurrence almost exclusively in the non-stone districts of East Anglia (Fig. 33 e) and Essex and in the chalk downland of Sussex is a clear indication that their employment was due to the local lack of freestone or even rubble for quoins, and the consequent adoption in a poor parish of a form which obviated the necessity for either. The form continued in use through the thirteenth century, and extended into the fourteenth century.

The form of covering adopted in Anglo-Norman towers is a question about which very little definite evidence survives. The west towers at Southwell[3] were crowned, down to the fire of 1711, by square pyramidal lead-covered roofs which may well represent the original twelfth-century covering, as it seems an unlikely form to have been adopted at any later period, when the octagonal form would probably have been preferred. These roofs were brought to the outer face of the walls, but that this was not always the case is proved by the survival at Norwich and elsewhere of angle-turrets which imply the confining of the covering within a parapet. The mid twelfth-century water-works drawing of Canterbury Cathedral shows a three-stage

---

[1] 130 examples have been noted in Norfolk, 40 in Suffolk, 6 in Essex, 3 in Sussex, 2 in Berks. and Cambs., and 1 in Surrey and Northants.

[2] *The Arts in Early England, Architecture*, 2nd edit., p. 423.

[3] See Hall and Hollar's engravings in Dugdale's *Monasticon*, 1673, iii, 'Secular Colleges', p. 10. The form has been reproduced in the existing modern roofs.

PLATE 11

DURHAM CASTLE, CHAPEL

1072

TOWER OF LONDON, ST. JOHN'S CHAPEL

late 11th century

PLATE 12

TEWKESBURY ABBEY, CENTRAL TOWER
c. 1140–50

TEWKESBURY ABBEY, W. FRONT
c. 1130–40

covering in the Carolingian manner over the central tower
and apparently pyramidal roofs over the western towers.
The pyramidal roof, furthermore, is shown as the conventional capping in twelfth-century manuscripts.

(*e*) *West Fronts*. The treatment of the west front of the
building depends upon the presence or absence of west
towers. Where no towers were designed, the front formed
the natural termination of the nave and aisles and was
finished with a main gable, and
sloping roofs to the aisles. The
best surviving front of this type is
at Rochester, where the main vertical divisions are emphasized by
turrets. A very similar front existed
till the end of the eighteenth century at Hereford. In both these
cases much of the wall-surfaces was
covered by arcading. At Tewkesbury (Pl. 12) the main division
of the front is occupied by an
enormous round arch of six orders,
forming a deep recess and rising

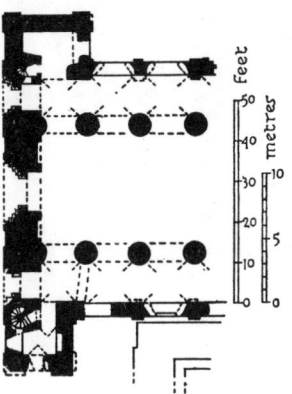

Fig. 20. St. Botolph's Priory,
Colchester. W. Front.

into the main gable. Foundations indicating a similar
arrangement have been found at Bath.

Twin west towers provide automatically an arrangement
which need not be particularized. Rich but ruined
examples of this type survive at Castle Acre Priory, Norfolk
(Pl. 24) and St. Botolph's Priory, Colchester (Fig. 20), but in
the latter case the towers are set beyond the aisles. The chief
surviving west front with a single axial tower is at Ely, where
a magnificent effect was produced by the addition of a
western transept, of which the northern arm has been largely
destroyed. This transept is finished with octagonal turrets,
each with eight ranges of arcading which are continued
along the end and sides. Even this elaborate front was,
however, eclipsed by that at Bury Abbey where the width

at the west end was some 250 ft. Of this only the ground plan and large masses of rubble core now survive.

(*f*) *Crypts*. The crypts of the greater English churches of the period form a remarkable group which is not a reflection of any correspondingly important feature in Normandy, though the crypt at Rouen[1] may well have served as a

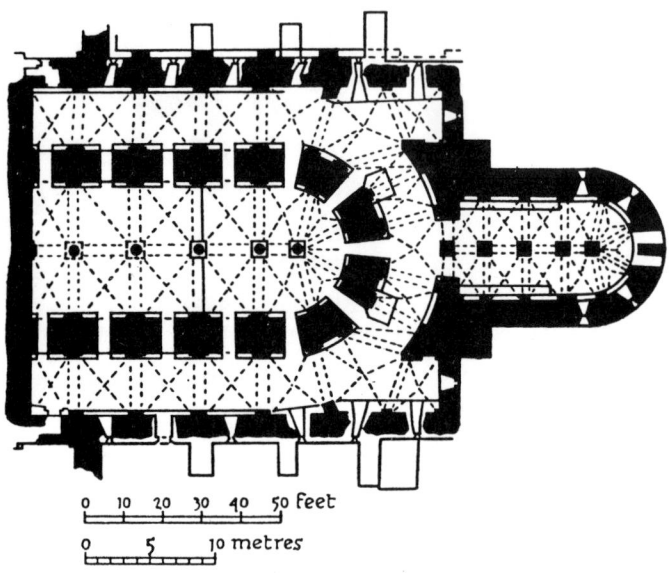

FIG. 21. Winchester Cathedral. Crypt.

model to the English builders. In addition to this example, small crypts are to be found under the choirs of the cathedral at Bayeux, and the Trinité at Caen,[2] but the second was not of the ambulatory plan. In England, with the exception of the example under Lanfranc's choir at Canterbury and the little eastern crypt at Christchurch,[3] these structures are all to be found under churches with an ambulatory. There are complete crypts of this type at Winchester (Fig. 21),[4] Gloucester, (Fig. 22)[5] and Worcester

[1] G. Lanfry in *Bull. de la soc. des amis des monuments rouennais*, 1924–5.
[2] *Congrès arch. de France* (Caen), i, p. 17.   [3] *V.C.H., Hants*, v, p. 100.
[4] Plan in Britton's *Cathedral Antiquities*, iii, and *V.C.H., Hants*, v, p. 52.
[5] Plan in *Bris. and Glos. Arch. Soc. Trans.*, 1876, p. 150.

PLATE 13

DURHAM CATHEDRAL, NAVE
finished c. 1130

WORCESTER CATHEDRAL, CRYPT
c. 1085

PLATE 14

CANTERBURY CATHEDRAL, WESTERN CRYPT
begun c. 1100

(Pl. 13),[1] an excavated example at St. Augustine's, Canterbury (Fig. 23),[2] and a fifth still awaits the spade at Bury St. Edmunds. All these are or were of similar type, and covered the same extent as the main building east of the crossing. At Winchester the two side-chapels are square-ended and are set axially east and west; at Worcester the

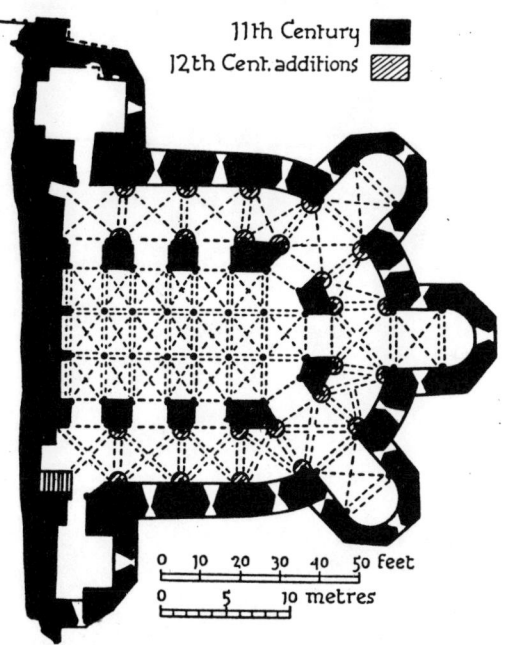

11th Century
12th Cent. additions

0 10 20 30 40 50 feet
0 5 10 metres

Fig. 22. Gloucester Cathedral. Crypt.

crypt does not extend under the radiating chapels, if such existed. The main span of these crypts is divided into two, three, or four aisles[3] by columns which support groined vaults under the floor of the presbytery above. To the same class belongs the crypt under the first eastern extension of the choir at Canterbury Cathedral (Pl. 14), built by Priors Ernulf and Conrad, but here the plan is

[1] Plan in *The Builder*, Aug. 1892.
[2] Plan in *Arch. Journ.*, lxxxvi, p. 278.
[3] Two aisles at Winchester, three at St. Augustine's, Canterbury and Gloucester, and four at Worcester.

complicated by the building of a second transept, and the subsequent further extension of the building in 1174–84.

The western part of the crypt at Rochester Cathedral has been generally assigned to Bishop Gundulph but, in spite of the early character of the columns, it seems more reasonable to connect it with an extension of the church under Bishop Ernulf. This crypt only begins at a point 30 ft. east of the crossing, which makes it difficult to reconcile it with

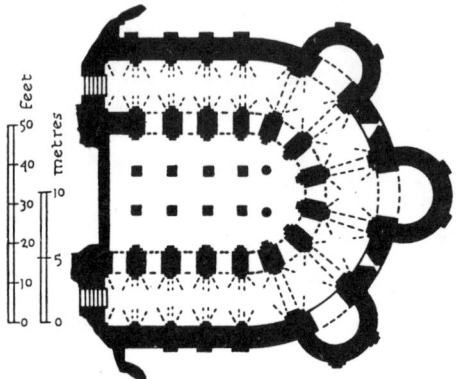

FIG. 23. St. Augustine's Abbey, Canterbury. Crypt.

the first plan, and it furthermore displays the use of Barnack stone which is not to be seen in any work that can be definitely assigned to Gundulph.

Two other early churches had crypts—old St. Paul's, the great width of which was remarked by William of Malmesbury, and Evesham Abbey,[1] which must have been largely extended when the square-ended ambulatory was built in the thirteenth century.

The construction of these early crypts appears to have been in no instance necessitated by a fall in the ground towards the east, as was the case at the Trinité at Caen, and it can only be supposed that the Anglo-Norman builders designed them either for the multiplication of chapels or for some other definite reason.

[1] *Chron. Abb. Evesham* (Rolls Ser.), p. 97.

PLATE 15

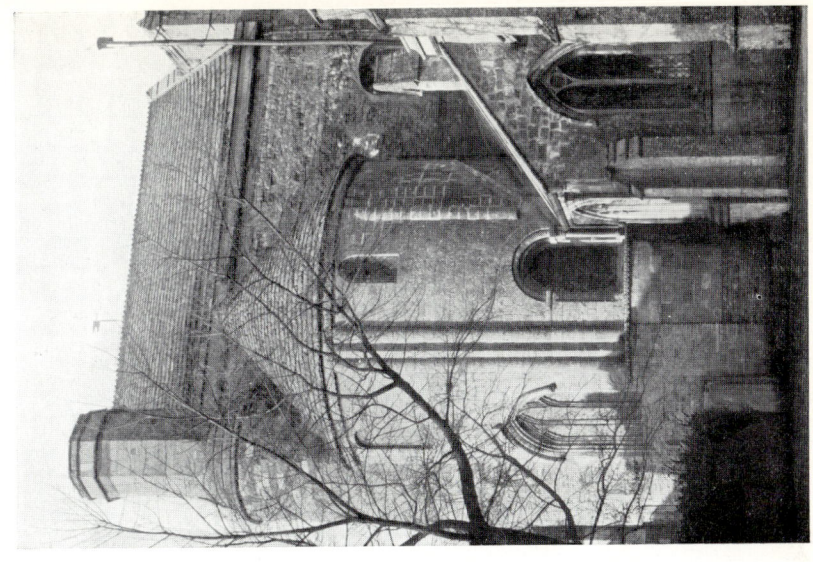

CHRISTCHURCH PRIORY, S. TRANSEPT

c. 1110

COLCHESTER CASTLE, DOORWAY

late 11th century

After the early part of the twelfth century they drop largely out of fashion except where the fall of the ground rendered them necessary, or the disturbance of a cemetery, by new building, rendered an ossuary or bone-hole desirable. An exception is to be found at York, where a large crypt (Fig. 29)[1] was built by Archbishop Roger under his extension (*c.* 1160–70).

The three small crypts under the choir and transepts of Flambard's church at Christchurch[2] stand in a class by themselves, and can perhaps be explained as a scheme for anchoring the whole building by exceptionally deep foundations at three fixed points.

In the lesser churches of the age crypts are uncommon, but good examples of early date survive under the choir at Lastingham,[3] *c.* 1078–88 (a cell of Whitby), under the church of St. Mary le Bow, London,[4] and under St. George's chapel in Oxford Castle.[5] Later crypts exist under the chancels of St. Peter in the East, Oxford,[6] St. Mary, Warwick,[7] and Berkswell[8] (Warwick), and under the north transept of Old St. Chad's at Shrewsbury.[9] The Hospitallers' church at Clerkenwell[10] has a crypt of *c.* 1140 enlarged late in the century, and another has been excavated at Temple Bruer[11] (Lincs.). A small example has recently been excavated under the destroyed church of Chilton Candover (Hants). At Lastingham the crypt is rendered necessary by the rapid fall of the ground.

(*g*) *Windows.* The simplest form of late eleventh- and twelfth-century window is a single round-headed light deeply splayed inside and with the splays brought almost to the external face of the wall. This is the common form

---

[1] J. Browne, *History of St. Peter's, York*, ii; *The Builder*, Jan. 7, 1893, and *Antiq. Journ.*, xi, p. 118.
[2] *V.C.H., Hants*, v, p. 101.   [3] *V.C.H., Yorks., N. Riding*, i, p. 526.
[4] *Roy. Com. on Hist. Mons., London*, iv, p. 79.   [5] *Arch. Journ.*, lxviii, p. 203.
[6] *Ibid.*   [7] *Ibid.*, lxxxiii, p. 302.   [8] *Birm. and Mid. Instit.*, x, p. 100.
[9] *Shropshire Arch. Soc. Trans.*, 2nd ser., ii, p. 359.
[10] *Roy. Com. on Hist. Mons., London*, ii, p. 17.   [11] *Arch.*, lxi, p. 177.

in village churches. Occasionally when the wall is of unusual thickness the double-splay window (generally a mark of pre-Conquest work) is found, as at Witham Friary (Somerset), Porchester keep, Lydford Castle (Devon), and Lewes Priory frater.[1] In the more important churches the single-light window is commonly provided with a recessed order to the jambs, either plain or containing a shaft supporting a moulded order to the arch. Additional light is provided not by making windows of two or more lights, in the Gothic manner, but by the grouping together of individual windows.[2] The round form of window is occasionally met with, generally in the clearstory, as at Southwell and Ledbury, and on a large scale in the ends of the east transept at Canterbury Cathedral. Wheel-windows with radiating shafts as spokes and arched heads to the lights, a favourite form in France, are very uncommon in England. There is a small late twelfth-century example at Barfreston (Kent), another in the neighbouring church of Patrixbourne, a third in the Temple church, London, and a fourth at Castle Hedingham (Essex). A large window in the same tradition but of early thirteenth-century date survives, in part, in the west front of Byland Abbey (Yorks.).

(h) *Doorways.* Hardly any of the main doorways of the late eleventh-century English churches have been suffered to survive unaltered, but a good idea of their former appearance can be gathered from the great entrance doorway[3] of Colchester Castle keep (Pl. 15), which dates from that period. Its round arch is of three roll-moulded orders and a label with billet ornament, while the mutilated side-

[1] A fifth example exists at Great Amwell Church (Herts.).

[2] In military and domestic work, on the other hand, windows of two lights divided by a free shaft are not uncommon, and this is the ordinary form for openings in the bell-chambers of parish-church towers.

[3] Recent excavation (1933) would seem to indicate that this doorway was an insertion, but even disregarding the early character of its mouldings and ornament, it formed the only entrance when the castle was temporarily finished off as a one-story building, before being carried up to its full height. *Roy. Com. on Hist. Mons., Essex,* iii, p. 51.

shafts have volute capitals of pure Norman type. The twelfth century saw an advance only in the number of the recessed orders of the arch and in their elaborate ornament. Fine examples may be seen at Castle Acre Priory (Pl. 24) (four orders), St. Botolph's Priory, Colchester (five orders), Tutbury Priory (Pl. 28),[1] Staffs. (six orders), and St. German's Priory, Cornwall (seven orders). In later examples these doorways were often set in a slight projection, to provide depth for additional orders, and finished with a gable.

It may be noted that, in contradistinction to those of pre-Conquest date, Norman doorways were always provided with a rebate or door-check.

(i) *Porches.* Porches were a very unusual adjunct, if, indeed, they existed at all, in Anglo-Norman churches of the eleventh century, and even in the twelfth century they were by no means common. A few, however, of the major churches of the first half of the twelfth century seem to have possessed them from the beginning, perhaps particularly those in which parishioners had rights over the nave of the building. The porch at Southwell (*c.* 1130) is remarkable in having a barrel-vault. The chamber above was approached from the triforium. Sherborne Abbey[2] (Dorset) retains a reconstructed porch of the same or rather later date with a ribbed vault and a modern superstructure.[3] A few of the larger parish churches also retain porches of this period.

---

[1] One order of this doorway is executed in alabaster, a very early example of the use of this material. For details see J. Potter, *Specimens of Ancient English Architecture,* 1848, Pls. 32–3.

[2] Canon C. H. Mayo, *Sherborne Abbey Church,* 1925.

[3] Bishop Roger's church at Old Sarum had a porch in a highly unusual position at the end of the south transept.

Chapter IV

THE REFORMED RELIGIOUS ORDERS

THE earliest church-building in England after the Conquest was largely in the hands of the Benedictine Order,
which drew its architectural inspiration, as we have seen,
almost entirely from Normandy. To this was soon to be
added, however, the influence of the reformed religious
orders, whose inspiration came from farther south. The
two most important of these orders, the Cluniac and the
Cistercian, owing largely to the influence of their two
greatest protagonists, St. Hugh of Cluny and St. Bernard of
Clairvaux, soon took up diametrically opposite positions
in the patronage of art. The Cluniacs consistently favoured
the view that no expense was too great to be lavished on the
structure and decoration of the church, whereas Cistercian
puritanism as sternly repressed all outward show as a vain
superfluity. Both orders drew their original inspiration from
Burgundy, the country alike of Cluny and Citeaux, but the
place of origin had more effect on Cistercian than on Cluniac
architecture in England. The foreign elements in both will
be considered in the sequel, together with the eventual
triumph of Cistercian simplicity which paved the way for
the transition to the Gothic style. The Order of Canons
Regular of St. Augustine with their reformed branch, the
Premonstratensian Canons, played only a subsidiary role in
the conflict of the opposing forces. In general they followed
the Cistercian lead rather than the Cluniac, but they have
certain features in addition which merit attention.

(a) *Cluniac.* The great church at Cluny,[1] actually the
third on the site, was begun in 1088 by St. Hugh and was
completed about thirty years later; the east end and three
of the radiating chapels were, however, finished by 1095.

[1] *Speculum* (Med. Acad. of America), iv, pp. 1 and 168; *Arch.*, lxxx, p. 143.

It was this vast structure, some 450 ft. long without the later narthex, which inaugurated the artistic achievements of the order not only in architecture but in decoration. It seems hardly yet proved that the splendid sculptured capitals of the main apse belong to the work completed in 1095, but in any case they are the foremost examples of Burgundian carving of that or the immediately succeeding age. The plan at Cluny is remarkable for the very striking innovation of the double transept, of which this is perhaps the earliest example.

The church was roofed with the barrel-vaults of the province, and the narthex, with which it was later provided, is also a distinctive feature of most of the larger churches of Burgundy. The effect of the building activity of Cluny is observable in its subordinate houses in France, of which La Charité-sur-Loire, Paray-le-Monial, Souvigny, and Nevers may be mentioned, and also in certain churches which came under its influence, such as Vézelay.

In England the first house of the order was at Lewes[1] (Sussex), founded by William de Warenne in 1077, and colonized direct from Cluny. This priory increased rapidly in wealth and importance, and was always the head of the order in this country. The plan of the church (Fig. 24) has been recovered by excavation and is, on a smaller scale, almost a replica of that at Cluny. Its history, however, presents certain difficulties. A dedication is recorded between the years 1091 and 1098, and a second between 1142 and 1147. It is difficult to believe that the whole church was laid out within a year or two, at most, of its model at Cluny; this argues an immediate contagion of ambitious ideas little in accord with the resources available; on the other hand, it is almost equally difficult to believe that the later dedication represents an enlargement on the precise model of a building which was already half

[1] W. H. St. J. Hope in *Sussex Arch. Colls.*, xxxiv, p. 71, and xlix, p. 66. See also W. H. Godfrey, *The Priory of St. Pancras at Lewes* (1927).

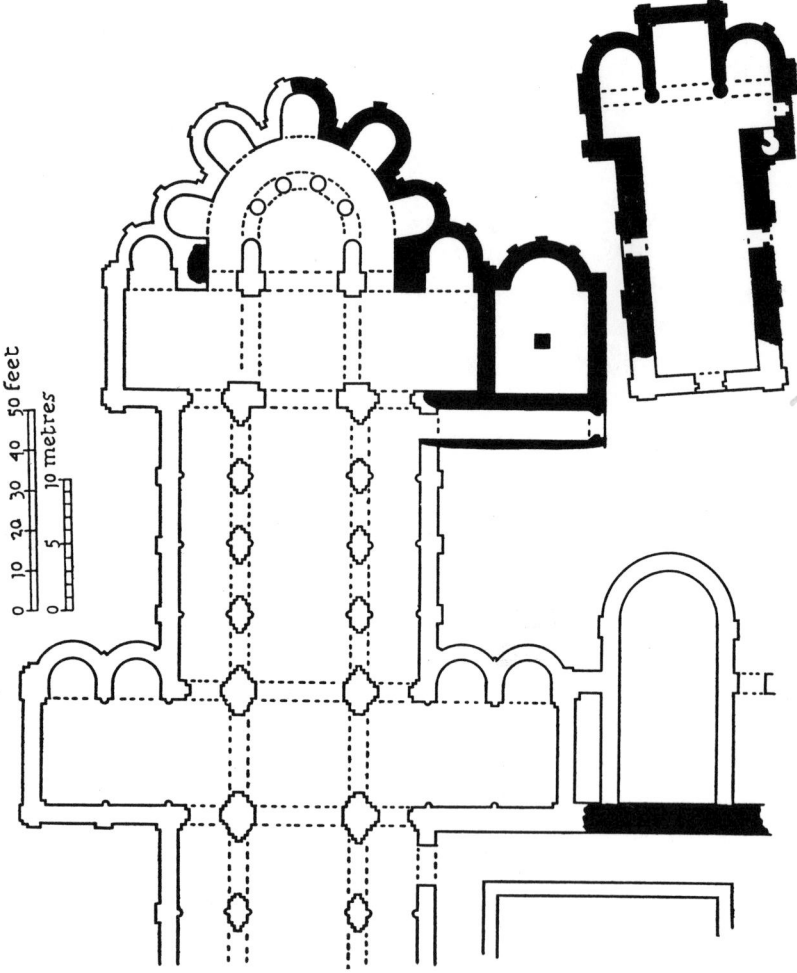

FIG. 24. Lewes Priory. Eastern parts of Church, &c.

a century old. In any case the completed church was a
smaller edition of the great church at Cluny, and the fragmentary remains of its sculptured decoration show certain
affinities with Burgundian work. The Cluny plan was not
copied, so far as we know, in any of the other Cluniac
churches in this country. Thetford[1] (founded on its present
site in 1107), Castle Acre[2] (founded *c.* 1089), and Much
Wenlock[3] (founded *c.* 1080) exhibited the normal three-
apse type of plan, while Monkton Farleigh[4] (founded *c.*
1120) appears to have had an ambulatory plan dating
from late in the twelfth century. A large fragment of Castle
Acre remains standing and displays an elaboration of ornament in full accord with Cluniac ideas, but not differing
from contemporary English work.[5]

We have seen that the early Anglo-Norman Benedictine
churches were extremely sparing in their decoration, but
after the opening years of the twelfth century this severity
gave place to a fondness for ornament which was only
restrained by the extent of the available funds. It seems not
unreasonable to assign this decorative impetus to some
extent to Cluniac example,[6] and it continued in increasing
force down to the dawn of the Gothic period. Thus the
break between the form and decoration of pure Romanesque and Gothic is a more sudden phenomenon in the
conservative orders of the Black Monks (Benedictines and

[1] F. H. Fairweather in *Ingleby's Sup. to Blomefield's Norfolk*, p. 334.
[2] W. H. St. J. Hope in *Norfolk Archaeology*, xii, p. 105, and F. H. Fairweather in
Sup. to Blomefield's Norfolk, p. 318.
[3] Dr. Cranage in *Arch.*, lxxii, p. 105.
[4] H. Brakspear in *Arch.*, lxxiii, p. 235.
[5] There are the remains of a rich west doorway at Monk's Horton Priory (Kent),
see *Arch. Journ.*, lxxxvi, p. 315; Bermondsey Abbey has produced some rather
elaborate and unusual capitals, see *Brit. Arch. Soc. Journ.*, 1926, p. 221, and *Roy.
Com. on Hist. Mons., London*, v, Pl. 18, and St. Andrew's Priory, Northampton,
had work of the same character, see *Journ. Northants N.H. Soc. Field Club*, xiii,
p. 79.
[6] Both Reading and Faversham abbeys, the royal foundations of Henry I and
Stephen, were colonized by Cluniac monks, though neither abbey belongs to
the order. For the series of elaborate capitals from Reading see *Proc. Soc. Ants.*
xxviii, 234.

Cluniacs) than amongst their rivals the White Monks (Cistercians) and their imitators. The latter were themselves responsible for the introduction of some of the most important features which led up to the change, so that with them its arrival was hardly apparent.

One other feature, already touched upon, of the church at Cluny was perhaps the origin of the double transept of so many of the great English churches of a later age. This double transept at Cluny was no doubt laid out in or soon after 1089. The first English church with a double transept was created by the extension of the choir at Canterbury, begun by Prior Ernulf (1096–1107). Here, as at Cluny, the eastern transept had a pair of apsidal chapels in each arm, and though the radiating chapels of the main apse are radically different in plan, the chronological sequence and the known influence of Cluny seem to give colour to the derivation. The double transept was repeated in Archbishop Roger's choir at York, in St. Hugh's rebuilding of Lincoln, begun in 1192, and in the later Gothic churches of Salisbury, York, Beverley, Worcester, and elsewhere.

(b) *Cistercian*.[1] The wide and rapid propagation of the Cistercian Order in the first half of the twelfth century was due almost entirely to the commanding personality of St. Bernard, Abbot of Clairvaulx (1115–53), who not only controlled its fortunes but identified the sternly reforming spirit of the order with his own puritanical views on art. The often quoted passage in his *Apologia* is a vivid exposition of the extreme Cistercian view of 'the immoderate length, superfluous breadth, costly polishing and strange designs' of the contemporary churches of other orders. As a consequence the early Cistercian churches were of the plainest possible description, from which all decoration, of whatever form, was strictly banished. Their length was con-

---

[1] John Bilson, 'The Architecture of the Cistercians, with special reference to some of their earlier churches in England', *Arch. Journ.*, lxvi, p. 185. S. Curman, *Cistercienserordens Byggnadskonst*, i (1912).

ditioned by their immediate needs, their height as low as
was convenient, their chancels and chapels square-ended as
being more economical to build and easier to roof than the
usual apsidal form; towers, furthermore, were prohibited by
a statute of the General Chapter of 1157. Within, they were
entirely unadorned, having neither paintings on the walls
nor coloured glass in the windows.

The architectural structure and detail of these early
buildings were (within the limits prescribed by these
Cistercian principles) those of the province of Burgundy
where the order took its rise. The abbey church of Fontenay[1] (Côte d'Or), the earliest surviving church of the
order in France, is typical of Cistercian building in the
simple and stereotyped form in which it was disseminated
throughout Europe. Fontenay was begun by Everard,
Bishop of Norwich, in 1139, and survives intact. On plan
it consists of a square-ended aisleless presbytery, transepts
with square eastern chapels divided by solid walls, and an
aisled nave; it has no structural crossing, and consequently
no central tower, and at the west end was a narrow narthex
extending the full width of the nave. The structure of
this building is purely Burgundian; the main spans are
covered by pointed barrel-vaults with ribs between the
bays; Cistercian feeling has excluded the triforium and the
barrel-vault precludes a clearstory. The aisles are covered
by a pointed barrel cross-vault in each bay, and the chapels
are similarly covered. The main arcades all have the
pointed arch, which by that time was usual in Burgundy,
but the door and window-heads are all semicircular.

Cistercian polity, by means of the annual general chapter
and the system of visitation of all daughter-houses by the
abbot of the mother-house at frequent intervals, was cal-
culated to maintain a greater cohesion and uniformity than
was then practicable in any other order. In addition there
seems no reason to doubt that, unlike other orders, the

---

[1] L. Bégule, *L'Abbaye de Fontenay et l'architecture cistercienne.*

Cistercian monks and lay-brothers took an active part in the design and construction of their buildings. Thus in several English abbeys, such as Byland and Jervaulx, the lay-brothers' quarters were the first buildings erected, no doubt to accommodate them while the rest of the monastery was building. As a consequence of these peculiarities, which endowed the Cistercian view of art with all the

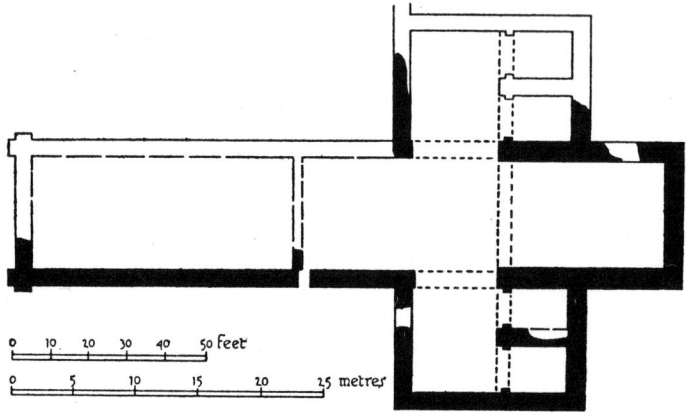

FIG. 25. Tintern Abbey. First Church.

advantages of a disciplined army over an unorganized opposition, Cistercian building throughout Europe presents in the twelfth century a remarkable similarity, both in plan and in intention.

The plan of Fontenay represents the type-plan which seems to have been carried with them wherever the Cistercians penetrated. In numerous cases the eastern arm was subsequently enlarged to provide more altars, and these enlargements were often varied in form with the country of their erection, but the original type remains largely unchanged in the great majority of churches dating from the middle of the twelfth century.

The Cistercians were first introduced into England by the foundation of the Abbey of Waverley[1] (Surrey) in 1128,

[1] H. Brakspear, *Waverley Abbey* (Surrey Arch. Soc.), 1905.

followed by the abbey of Tintern[1] (Mon.) in 1131 (Fig. 25). At both these places the plans have been recovered of the first churches on their respective sites, and these appear to represent an earlier type than that of Fontenay, of which there are now no survivals in France. Both churches were cruciform, square-ended, and had aisleless naves; they differ only in that Waverley had one chapel only in each arm of the transept while Tintern had two.

The earliest church of the normal Cistercian type which has left any remains is Rievaulx[2] (Yorks.) founded in 1132 (seven years before the building of Fontenay), and a daughter house of Clairvaulx. Here (Fig. 26) the transepts survive, and recent excavations have recovered the plan and much of the structure of the nave. Following this comes Fountains[3] (Yorks.), begun about 1135, Kirkstall[4] (Yorks.), begun about 1152, and Buildwas[5] (Salop), begun about 1155–60. These churches provide the best preserved and earliest examples of Cistercian building in England. All present the typical Cistercian plan[6] described above (with a very minor modification at Fountains) and all are without a triforium. The pointed Burgundian form is used in all the main arches while the semicircular form is retained for doors and windows. At Rievaulx and Fountains (Pl. 18) the pointed barrel transverse vaults of Burgundy are used over the aisles of the nave and they appear also in the chapels at Kirkstall, but after that they disappear for good. At Rievaulx[7] they are evidently a direct importation, for here the nave piers are square and the cross-vaults are

[1] H. Brakspear, *Tintern Abbey* (O. of W. Guide), 2nd edit., 1929.
[2] C. R. Peers, *Rievaulx Abbey* (O. of W. Guide), 1928.
[3] W. H. St. J. Hope, 'Fountains Abbey', in *Yorks. Arch. Journ.*, xv, p. 274.
[4] W. H. St. J. Hope, 'Kirkstall Abbey', in *Publ. of Thoresby Soc.*, xvi.
[5] *The Builder*, Oct. 1900.
[6] This plan was also adopted, with little modification, in the abbeys of Bindon, Bordesley, Calder, Cleeve, Dore (before the extension), Hulton, Louth Park, Newminster, Quarr, Sawtrey, Strata Florida, Valle Crucis, Whitland, and probably also at Boxley and Merevale.
[7] None of these arches is now standing, but sufficient survived, where it had fallen, to permit the reconstruction of the whole arrangement.

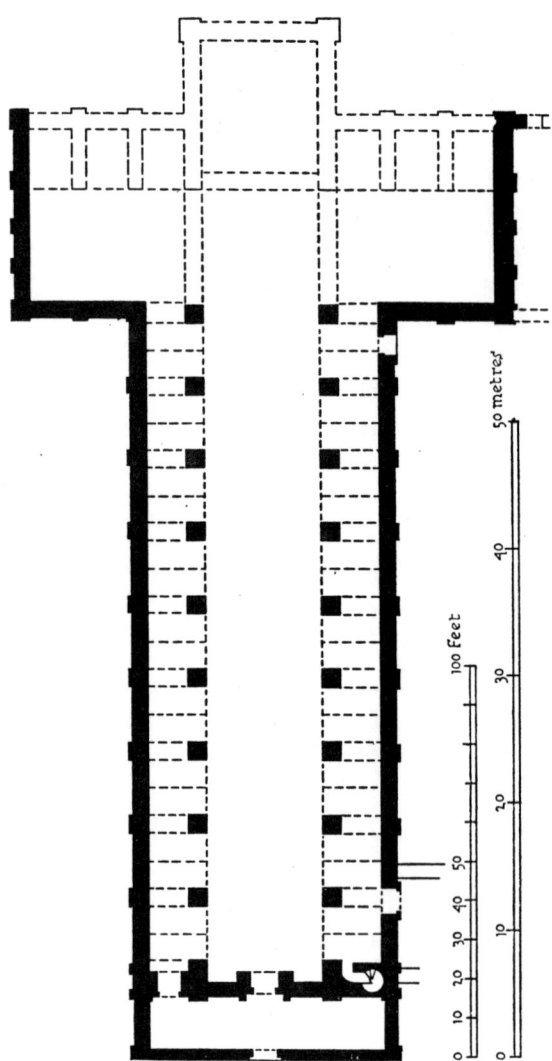

FIG. 26. RIEVAULX ABBEY. First Church.

continuations of the arches of the nave arcades, an arrangement which is unique in England. So far the structure of these churches follows that of the parent country, but otherwise this structure is largely dictated by the established fashions of Anglo-Norman Romanesque. Thus no attempt was ever made to erect a barrel-vault over the main spans.[1] In England a clearstory was a necessity, and to provide for it the main spans were either roofed with timber or with a ribbed vault. Such ribbed vaults, so far as we know, were confined in these churches to the chancel; they remain intact at Kirkstall, and have left traces at Buildwas. In both these cases they are found in connexion with the pointed arch, an association which endows them with a special significance. This use of the pointed arch in a ribbed vault was the final and culminating step in the development of the Gothic vault, and the vault at Kirkstall is, with the exception of the nave-vault at Durham, perhaps the earliest example surviving in England. The system did not come with the Cistercians from Burgundy, where it was not adopted till a later date. It was, on the other hand, already in use (since about 1130) in the Ile de France. The vault at Kirkstall, however, shows certain differences in structure from those of the Ile de France which inclined Dr. John Bilson to consider that it was a development of the Anglo-Norman ribbed vault used in connexion with the Cistercian pointed arch rather than inspired by the French work.

In spite of the actual prohibition of bell-towers and their general absence in French Cistercian churches, the English building tradition was too strong to be resisted, and though there is no provision for one at Rievaulx, the rather later English Cistercian churches such as Fountains, Kirkstall, and Buildwas all had the four arches to the crossing and a low central tower. Among the French Cistercians the early practice seems to have been to carry the nave roof

[1] Unless the increased thickness of the side wall of the chancel of the first church at Tintern was intended to support a barrel-vault.

east without a break to the chancel arch and for the chancel and transepts to be roofed at a rather lower level. This system was adopted very generally in Irish Cistercian houses,[1] and it is the more remarkable that there is no certain instance of its employment in England.

At the west end of all the earliest Cistercian churches was the narrow narthex referred to above. This was a well-known Burgundian feature, much restricted and brought within bounds by Cistercian repression. There are (partly reconstructed) remains of this feature at Fountains and Rievaulx; it had a timber pent-roof, and an open arcade, like that of a cloister, towards the west.

The clearstory consists generally of a single round-headed window in each bay without a wall-passage. There are a number of instances, elsewhere in the building, of the round form of window-opening, as in the chapels at Fountains and originally in the east gable at Kirkstall. This was a favourite Cistercian form, to be subsequently used on a large scale in the west front at Byland (Yorks.).

The last quarter of the twelfth century saw the erection in England of a number of Cistercian churches in which the typical plan was abandoned or modified and the structural system was altered and elaborated. The most important of these are Byland[2] (Yorks.), begun about 1175 (Fig. 27), Roche[3] (Yorks.), begun a little earlier (Fig. 28), Furness[4] (Lancs.), begun c. 1175, and Jervaulx[5] (Yorks.), begun about 1175. Of these Roche and Furness adhered to the general lines of the earlier plan, but abandoned the solid walls between the chapels. Byland, a complete church on a new site, adopted a plan with an aisle to the presbytery

[1] *Arch. Journ.* lxxxviii, p. 20.
[2] C. R. Peers, *Byland Abbey* (O. of W. Guide), 1929.
[3] Plan in *Yorks. Arch. Soc. Excursion Prog.*, 1887.
[4] W. H. St. J. Hope, 'Abbey of St. Mary in Furness', in *Cumb. and Westmorland Arch. Soc. Trans.* xvi.
[5] W. H. St. J. Hope and H. Brakspear, 'Jervaulx Abbey', in *Yorks. Arch. Journ.*, xxi, p. 303.

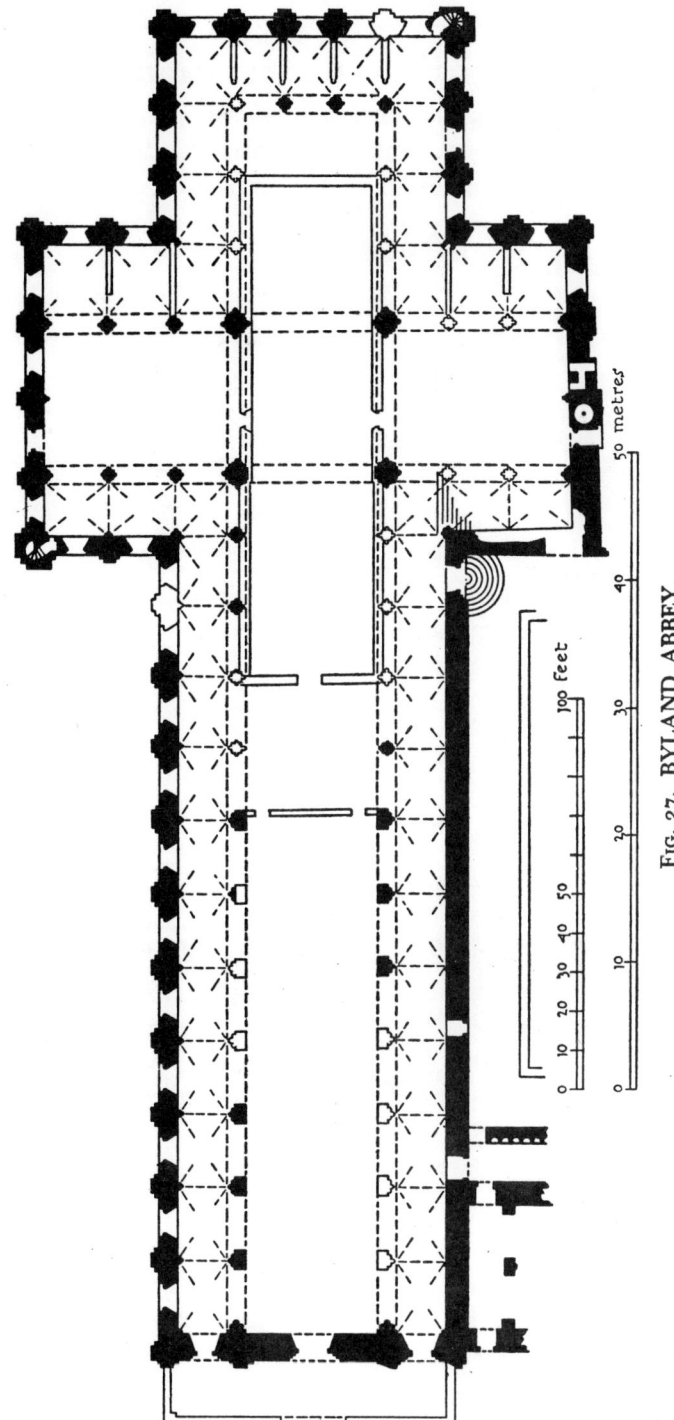

FIG. 27. BYLAND ABBEY.

M

returned round the east end, which was pierced by arches opening into it. At Jervaulx[1] the main arcades of the aisled presbytery were continued to the extreme east end of the

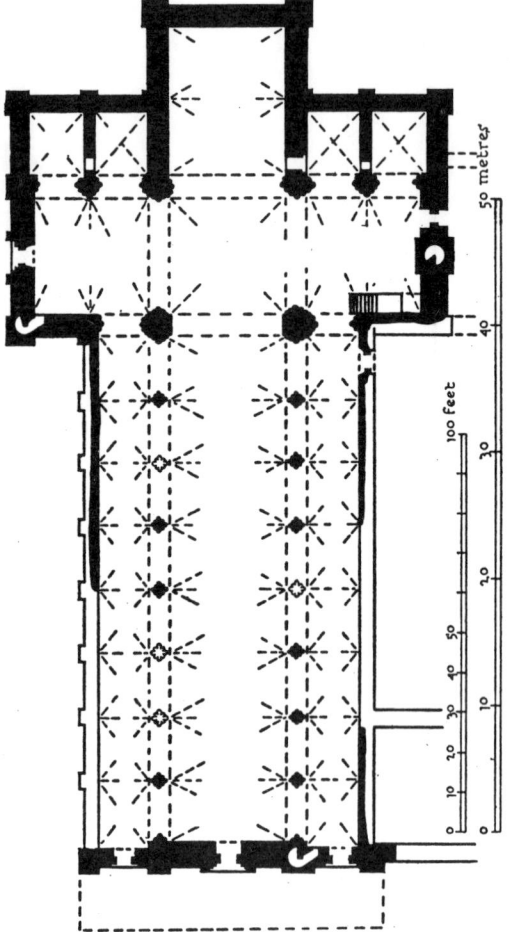

FIG. 28. Roche Abbey.

building without a structural ambulatory or chapel-aisle. In other matters too these churches show a break away from earlier traditions. At both Roche and Byland there is a return to the triforium-story, and in the first church the

---

[1] The presbytery was not completed until early in the thirteenth century.

surviving parts show evidence of a complete system of ribbed vaulting in stone.

The Cistercians seem to have been the first in England to adopt the corbel (a Burgundian motif) as a means of support to the springers of a vault, instead of carrying the vaulting-shafts down to the ground. It had the advantage of leaving more space for circulation in the aisles of a building, and incidentally of reducing the cost.

The ornament of these English Cistercian churches is generally confined to the capitals of the columns and shafts and to certain doorways. Many of these details show only a restricted use of the motives then current in Anglo-Norman Romanesque; such are the scalloped capitals at Fountains, Kirkstall, and Buildwas, or the more elaborate west doorway at Kirkstall, but the Cistercians early evinced a preference for the simple leaf-form as a decoration for the capital, and this was applied to a simple bell-capital, which seems to have been an introduction from France. These leaves are commonly of the type known as water-leaf, and often form a small scroll at the angle. In the matter of mouldings, while their use is more sparing in Cistercian building than elsewhere, in form they followed the general course of development in English building of the period.

The English and Welsh Cistercian churches founded in the twelfth century numbered sixty-three, scattered fairly evenly over the country. Each, no doubt, became a centre of local influence, and did its part in the introduction and propagation of those ideas which were in time to bring Romanesque art to an end and supplant it by the full Gothic style.

(c) *Canons Regular*. The Canons Regular of St. Augustine were introduced into this country about the beginning of the twelfth century, and possessed eventually a larger number of houses than any other religious order. Most of these, however, were small and poorly endowed, and consequently had little architectural opportunity. Among the greater houses it is interesting to see the effect of the conflicting influences of the Cluniac and Cistercian schools on what may be considered a neutral body. As might be expected, the earliest churches of the order display the same architectural taste as the Cluniac and Benedictine builders, but as the century advances their churches approximate more and more to Cistercian standards, as the influence of that order gradually augmented. In the Augustinian Order, however, there was no standard plan, and its buildings present a greater variety than those of any other body. It is thus only in a general way or in certain individual instances that outside influences can be traced. The ambulatory plan of St. Bartholomew Smithfield[1] (c. 1123), the enriched front of St. Botolph at Colchester[2] (c. 1120), and the elaborate chapter-house of St. Augustine Bristol[3] (a very close copy of the Cluniac chapter-house at Wenlock), all belong to the older school, whereas the pure Cistercian plan at Lesnes[4] (Kent) founded 1189, shows evident traces of the later influence.

The reformed Order of Canons Regular, called Premonstratensian Canons,[5] was both in its founding and constitution so closely akin to the Cistercian Order that its architecture followed perforce in the same channel. The largest surviving Premonstratensian church in France—S. Martin at Laon—is a close copy of the standard Cistercian plan except that it was provided with towers and had no narthex. In England the remains of the twelfth-century churches of this order are slight, but are yet sufficient to show a general plan approximating to the Cistercian except for the common absence of aisles to the nave. A church of almost purely Cistercian type survives in part at Talley Abbey (Glam.).

[1] E. A. Webb in *Arch.*, lxiv, p. 165.
[2] C. R. Peers, *St. Botolph's Priory, Colchester* (O. of W. Guide).
[3] R. Paul in *Arch.*, lxiii, p. 231.   [4] A. W. Clapham, *Lesnes Abbey* (1915).
[5] A. W. Clapham in *Arch.*, lxxiii, p. 117.

Chapter V

LATE TWELFTH-CENTURY BUILDING

WE have traced in the first two chapters the course of Anglo-Norman building in the eleventh and the first half of the twelfth century, and in the last chapter the new architectural ideas which were introduced by the Cistercians, and it now remains to consider the final phase, occupying the last half of the century, in which Romanesque finally gave place to Gothic.

The advent to the throne of Henry II marked the beginning of a more prosperous era in which firm government and settled conditions reacted most favourably on the building arts. The second half of the twelfth century was thus a period of considerable architectural activity not only in England but also in France, where an extraordinary outburst of popular religious enthusiasm gave the necessary impetus for the early flowering of full Gothic in the Ile de France. It is not within the scope of this chapter to trace the rise of Gothic in the royal domain of the French crown, however much this may have affected English work, but rather to pursue the gradually retreating features of Romanesque until their final and almost total eclipse at the close of the century. The mingling of Romanesque and Gothic forms, which the older writers called the Transitional style, was not in England a universal phase of development; here and there churches continued to be built in which most of the traditional Romanesque features were retained, with all the most florid types of Romanesque ornament. The old style in many places died hard, and we are occasionally confronted, as in the west front at Ely, with the juxtaposition of full Romanesque with mature Gothic without any intermediate stage, and with hardly any appreciable interval.

It has been said that true Gothic consists of the organic use of the pointed arch, the ribbed vault, and the flying buttress, and this is true if the flying buttress be taken as the symbol of a system of transmitting stresses from a higher to a lower point of the structure. We have seen how the Anglo-Norman school was amongst the first to adopt the ribbed vault and also how the Cistercians popularized the pointed arch, combining it with the ribbed vault; it was not, however, until the second half of the twelfth century that any progress was made in England towards the general adoption of the buttress as a definite means of transmitting thrusts. The earlier builders depended almost entirely on the thickness of their walls, feebly reinforced by pilaster buttresses save in the few instances where the abutting arches or vault of the triforium served the purpose of a flying buttress. In France these abutting arches or vaults formed the germ from which the flying buttress was gradually perfected, but after an occasional early and sometimes abortive attempt in England the problem slumbered for a generation, and its solution was not even attempted by the early Cistercians. This was due, perhaps, to a national caution which led to the retention in the vast majority of cases of the timber covering, and it was not until the last quarter of the century that, among the great English churches, the complete system of stone vaulting became the general rule and timber ceilings the exception.

Before proceeding to examine the plan and structure of these late twelfth-century churches it will be necessary to give some particulars of the more important surviving examples.

Malmesbury Abbey[1] church (Benedictine) was begun about 1145, but the surviving portion—the nave—dates from about 1160. It is an aisled building of nine bays with cylindrical columns, pointed arches, and stone vaults to the aisles only, the main vault being a later addition. It is the

[1] H. Brakspear, 'Malmesbury Abbey', *Arch.* lxiv, p. 399.

earliest building in which Sir H. Brakspear[1] has found some of the peculiarities of a west-country school of masons to which he assigns much subsequent work.

York Cathedral[2] choir (secular) was rebuilt by Archbishop Roger Pont-l'Evêque[3] (1154–81). Nothing now remains of it except the lower part of the walls of the crypt (Fig. 29),

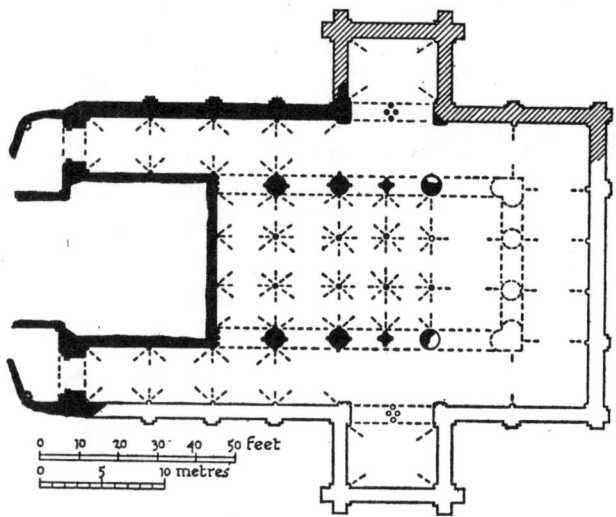

FIG. 29. York Minster. Crypt.

which show that it was an aisled building most probably with a square end and ambulatory beyond and with projecting chapels forming an eastern transept. Its details indicate that it was begun about 1160–65.

Canterbury Cathedral[4] (Fig. 16) choir (Benedictine) was rebuilt after the fire of 1174 under the French master, William of Sens (1174–84), followed by William the Englishman, who completed the work. An exact account of the operations from year to year by a monk of the convent, Gervase of Canterbury, is a remarkable document without a parallel

[1] Sir H. Brakspear in *Arch.*, lxxxi, p. 1.
[2] J. Browne, *History of St. Peter's, York*, ii; R. Willis, 'The Architecture of York Minster', in *Proc. R. Arch. Inst.* (York), 1846; *Antiq. Journ.*, xi, p. 118.
[3] R. Twysden, *Decem Scriptores* (Thomas Stubbs), p. 1723.
[4] R. Willis, *Architectural History of Canterbury Cathedral*, 1845.

in English architectural history of the Middle Ages. The retention of much of the outer walls of the earlier structure necessitated the curious contracting plan of the eastern extension, which is provided with an ambulatory and a circular eastern chapel (Pl. 17). The whole is vaulted in stone. The earlier crypt was continued under the whole of the extension.

Glastonbury Abbey[1] (Benedictine) was burnt to the ground in 1184, and the reconstruction began with the building of

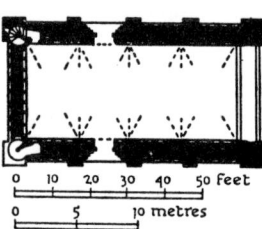

FIG. 30. Glastonbury.
Lady Chapel.

the new Lady Chapel (Pl. 16) on the site of the timber *vetusta ecclesia* traditionally dedicated by Christ to His Virgin Mother. This rectangular chapel (Fig. 30) was built between the years 1184 and 1186. The great church was begun to the east of it, probably about 1186 and continued to the transept with some rapidity; the nave, however, was not finished until much later. The choir was square-ended, with aisles and an ambulatory, and the transept had an eastern aisle with a range of chapels beyond it. The whole building appears to have been vaulted.

Ripon Minster (secular)[2] was rebuilt by Archbishop Roger Pont-l'Evêque (1154–81), who gave £1,000[3] for building the church 'which we have begun afresh'. The different and much more advanced character of this church as compared with the same archbishop's new choir at York indicates that it cannot have been begun much before 1180. It consisted of an aisled choir, perhaps with an ambulatory beyond the square east end, transepts, and an aisleless nave of unusual width (40 ft.). The east end was rebuilt at a later date, and only the two ends of the nave survive the subsequent addition of aisles to this part of the building.

[1] Armitage Robinson in *Arch. Journ.*, lxxxv, p. 18. Plan in *ibid.*, lxxxvii, p. 440.
[2] Sir G. Scott in *Arch. Journ.*, xxxi, p. 310; *The Builder*, Feb. 1893.
[3] *Memorials of Ripon* (Surtees Soc.), i, p. 97.

PLATE 16

BUILDWAS ABBEY, NAVE
c. 1160

GLASTONBURY ABBEY, LADY CHAPEL
1184–6

PLATE 17

DOVER CASTLE KEEP, UPPER CHAPEL
c. 1181

CANTERBURY CATHEDRAL, E. END
c. 1180–4

Chichester Cathedral[1] (secular). A destructive fire in 1186 led to the rebuilding of the choir of Chichester between that year and 1199, when the new building was consecrated. The aisles are continued beyond the main gable-wall of the choir, and flank a pre-existing Lady Chapel. The nave was reconditioned at the same period.

Wells Cathedral[2] (secular). The new church was begun about 1190, and proceeded slowly from east to west. The east end was square, with an ambulatory, but has been destroyed by the subsequent extension, only the side walls and aisles surviving. The transepts have east and west aisles. The church was completely vaulted in stone, and is perhaps the earliest large church in England in which practically all traces of Romanesque design and detail are lost.

Lincoln Cathedral[3] (secular). The rebuilding of this cathedral was begun in 1192[4] when the bishop, St. Hugh, laid the first stone; a certain Geoffrey de Noiers[5] was constructor or architect. Here again there is little or no trace of Romanesque save in the plan. The east end (Fig. 31), now destroyed, was a three-sided apse with a range of apsidal and polygonal chapels grouped round it. The eastern or lesser transept still retains its apsidal chapels.

In addition to the major churches mentioned above a large number of secondary churches were built or rebuilt during the same period. Mention may be made of St. Cross, Winchester[6] (secular Hospital), begun about 1160; Orford, Suffolk[7] (parochial), the fragment of a large church

[1] R. Willis, *Chichester Cathedral*.

[2] Armitage Robinson and John Bilson in *Arch. Journ.*, lxxxv, p. 1.

[3] *Arch. Journ.*, xliv, p. 194.

[4] The earlier cathedral had been 'split from top to bottom' by an earthquake in 1185 (*Gest. Reg. Hen. secundi Benedicti abbatis* (Rolls Ser.), i, p. 337); the first stone of the new cathedral was laid in 1192 (*Irish Arch. Soc. Tracts*, ii, 'Annales Monte Fernandi', p. 11).

[5] *Mag. Vit. S. Hugonis* (Rolls Ser.), p. 336.   [6] *V.C.H., Hants*, v, p. 59.

[7] Recent excavations (1931) by Dr. Fairweather have determined the plan of the destroyed east end, which was square and extended one bay beyond the aisles.

built about 1166; St. Frideswide, Oxford[1] (Austin Canons, now the Cathedral), and Worksop Priory[2] nave (Austin Canons), both about 1180; the Temple Church, London,[3] round nave dedicated in 1185; Brinkburn Priory[4] (Austin Canons), and New Shoreham, Sussex[5] (parochial), both of about 1180–90.

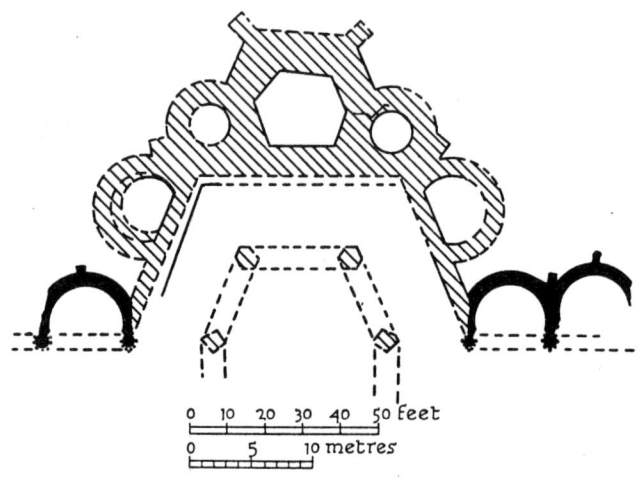

0 10 20 30 40 50 feet
0   5   10 metres

FIG. 31. Lincoln. E. end of St. Hugh's Church.

Plan. The apsidal east end with or without an ambulatory was generally abandoned in this period, though the ambulatory plan has been surmised at Malmesbury, and was retained at Canterbury owing to the inclusion of much of the earlier building and probably also to the French influence of William of Sens. St. Hugh's three-sided apse at Lincoln (now destroyed), though bearing some slight resemblance to the extended choir of Canterbury, is in a class by itself and, so far as we know, was never imitated in this country.

The favourite form of east end for the larger churches

[1] *The Builder*, June 1892, and R. Willis in *Arch. Journ.*, vii, p. 315.
[2] *Assoc. Archit. Socs. Reports*, v, p. 208.
[3] *Roy. Com. on Hist. Mons., London*, iv, p. 137.
[4] *County Hist. of Northumberland*, vii, p. 478.
[5] E. Sharpe, *Arch. Hist. of St. Mary's Church, New Shoreham.*

would seem to have been the square end with the ambulatory beyond it, which, as we have seen, was adopted at Romsey Abbey as early as about 1120. To this type belonged Archbishop Roger's choir at York, perhaps his choir at Ripon, Glastonbury Abbey, and Wells Cathedral. Chichester choir also belongs to the same class, though here there is no free passage beyond the main east wall.

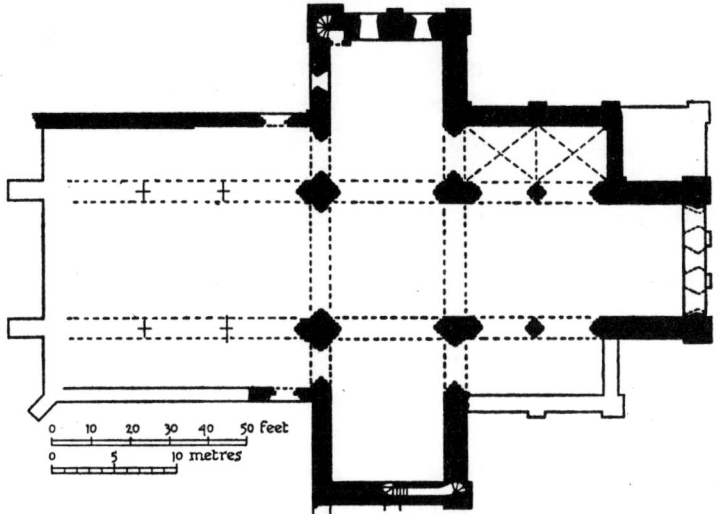

FIG. 32. Cartmel Priory. Lancs.

A curious variation of the ambulatory plan is to be found in the extension probably built by Bishop William de Vere (1186–1200) at Hereford (Fig. 15);[1] here the added ambulatory beyond the Norman east end took the form of an eastern transept with two chapels in each arm and a central projecting chapel of unknown length.

Side by side with the ambulatory plan appears a new type which in the next century was to become almost universal in the great English churches. This was the square east end with the main arcades and high roofs carried up to it. In the twelfth century this type was

[1] *Roy. Com. on Hist. Mons., Herefordshire*, i, p. 101.

apparently confined to the lesser churches. It makes an early appearance at St. Cross at Winchester, begun about 1160, and was occasionally followed in some of the larger parish churches, such as New Shoreham (Sussex), *c.* 1180–90.

A third form, with the square-ended presbytery extending a bay or more beyond the aisles, was the favourite type in the churches of the Austin Canons. Such choirs were built at St. Frideswide Priory, Oxford[1] (now the cathedral), Little Dunmow Priory[2] (Essex), Cartmel Priory (Fig. 32)[3] (Lancs.), and at the parish church at Orford (Suffolk).

A further innovation was the addition of a large axial Lady Chapel at the end of the church. This pre-existed the rebuilding of the choir at Chichester and was foreshadowed at Old Sarum in the rebuilding by Bishop Roger. A late twelfth-century Lady Chapel was added to the east end of Great Malvern Priory.[4] Owing to special circumstances the Lady Chapels at Glastonbury and Durham[5] (the Galilee) were built at the west end of the church, the former to equate with the site of the *vetusta ecclesia*, and the latter because an earlier attempt to build the chapel at the east end had failed. Glastonbury Lady Chapel (Pl. 16) is of great value in being exactly dated to the years 1184–6, and the Galilee at Durham is unique as consisting of five equal and parallel aisles; it was a work of Bishop Hugh de Puiset, and may be dated *c.* 1175.

The aisleless nave of Roger's church at Ripon is a very unusual feature for a church of its size and importance. It was provided with a main range of windows and a clearstory above, and may be compared with the much smaller but very elaborate nave of the Benedictine nunnery of

---

[1] *The Builder,* June 1892.
[2] *Essex Arch. Soc. Trans.,* N.S., xiii, p. 285, and *Roy. Com. on Hist. Mons., Essex,* i, p. 175.
[3] *The Builder,* Oct. 1899.
[4] *V.C.H., Worcestershire,* iv, p. 129.
[5] *V.C.H., Durham,* iii, p. 119.

Nun Monkton[1] near York. This is perhaps of two periods, the upper part being slightly later in date than the nave at Ripon; the west doorway, though dating from late in the twelfth century, has more definitely Romanesque features than anything surviving at Ripon. In this connexion it is curious to compare the rich but almost entirely Romanesque details of Roger's crypt at York with the almost Cistercian severity of his later work at Ripon.

Structure. The structure of the late twelfth-century churches shows almost as much variety as their plan. In the earlier examples the general scheme is often in direct descent from the buildings of the time of Henry I. Thus the nave of Malmesbury (*c.* 1160) maintains the traditional west-country use of the cylindrical pier with the adoption, however, of the pointed arch. The ribbed vaults of the aisles were the only parts not covered by timber ceilings, and the triforium retains the form and importance of the previous age. The ornament throughout is of Romanesque character. In the slightly later church at Orford the arches are all semicircular; the aisles had ribbed vaults and the main span of the chancel was very likely also covered by a stone vault. Though on a small scale, it must have been a very complete example of almost pure Romanesque, only betraying its advanced date by the profiles of its mouldings. Steyning church[2] (Sussex) shows an equal attachment to the earlier forms, while the nave of St. John's at Chester, which (from the base-mouldings) cannot be earlier than 1175, has massive cylindrical piers (5¼ ft. diam.) and heavy round arches of three square unmoulded orders. The more advanced triforium and still later clearstory show that nothing more than a timber roof was ever contemplated.

Perhaps the richest of these almost pure late Romanesque buildings was Archbishop Roger's choir at York. Only the merest ruin of his crypt remains, but its elaborate

[1] W. Richardson, *Monastic Ruins of Yorks.*, ii, p. 83; *The Churches of Yorkshire* (1845), ii, p. 90. [2] *Sussex N. and Q.*, iv, p. 211.

ornament is of extraordinary richness and variety. Here we meet, perhaps for the first time, a pier composed of four free and equal shafts, and many of the other details are almost equally unusual. A little contemporary work of the same character can be seen in the vestibule of the chapter-house of St. Mary's Abbey in the same city.

The Galilee at Durham is another and notable example of this late Romanesque type of building. It was, as we have seen, erected by Bishop Hugh de Puiset perhaps about 1175 and its five equal aisles have slender twin columns[1] and semicircular arches; throughout it is of one story only.

Into the midst of this late flowering Romanesque, which only here and there had been influenced by Cistercian example, was transplanted the first genuinely Gothic building—the new choir of Canterbury.

The building of this extended choir at Canterbury between 1174 and 1184, introduced into England if not a new system of construction at least an example of that early Gothic system which had already achieved its first triumphs in the Ile de France. The general design of the Canterbury extension must be assigned to the French master, William of Sens, who directed the work for the first four years of its progress, being succeeded by William the Englishman. The building falls naturally into its place in the chronological sequence of early Gothic churches of the Ile de France,[2] and displays certain features which had hitherto been unrepresented in England. One of the earliest of these French churches was the cathedral of Sens, the native town of the master mason of Canterbury. This church was begun rather before 1140, and was roofed with a series of sexpartite vaults over double bays, with composite major piers and coupled cylindrical minor piers. The same sexpartite system was employed at Senlis Cathedral, begun about 1155, and at Laon Cathedral, begun slightly later. At

---

[1] Two more shafts were added to each pier at a later date.
[2] R. de Lasteyrie, *L'Architecture religieuse en France à l'époque gothique*, i, chap. 2.

the last place, however, the arcade piers are uniform, the double bays being separated only by heavier vaulting-shafts. The abandonment of these heavier shafts is seen at Notre Dame at Paris, begun in 1163, where the bays throughout are of uniform elevation, though the sexpartite vault over each pair of bays is retained. It was at this point that the architects of the Ile de France had arrived when William of Sens was called upon to rebuild the choir of Canterbury. He designed a building in full conformity with the traditions of his school. The pointed arch is almost universally employed in the main features, the vault is in sexpartite double bays and is supported by flying buttresses which appear above the triforium roof. The internal bays are of nearly uniform elevation, and the main arches rest on cylindrical piers. The piers of the main eastern extension or Trinity chapel are of coupled cylindrical form like the subsidiary piers at Sens, though this part of the building at Canterbury was actually erected under William the Englishman.

The sexpartite vault at Canterbury is the first example of its type in England and hardly found an imitator,[1] as it was introduced at a time when this form was already going out of fashion in the Ile de France in favour of the much more stable and convenient system of an oblong quadripartite vault over each bay.[2] This form both preceded and succeeded the sexpartite vault, the earlier examples being handicapped by the absence of an effective key-stone. The difficulty of butting the rib voussoirs at the intersection of the diagonal ribs in an oblong vault without an effective key-stone led to the adoption of the square bay in which the diagonal ribs meet at right-angles, thus reducing any tendency to dislocation at this point. This square bay was

---

[1] A sexpartite vault in the enriched Romanesque manner exists over the chancel of Tickencote church (Rutland), and may perhaps date from c. 1160–70.

[2] A curious return to an older system is to be seen in the vault (c. 1190) of the choir of Boxgrove Priory (Sussex), which is of quadripartite form over a double bay. *The Builder's Journal*, April 1904, and *Sussex Arch. Colls.*, lxi, p. 18.

obtained by making one double bay of the main vault equate with two bays of the aisles. The gradual evolution and adoption of a key-stone of sufficient size to avoid risk of dislocation or fracture, and comprising not only the junctions of the ribs but a section of the web surrounding them, overcame the difficulty and led to the general abandonment of the sexpartite vault.[1]

Thus the choir at Canterbury occupies a curiously isolated position as an example of early French Gothic transplanted into Kent. This applies, however, only to its general design; in detail it reproduces some of the English features of ornament which were current at the period, and it is perhaps the earliest English building in which the Romanesque cheveron and the Gothic dog-tooth appear side by side.

The building at Canterbury seems to have had some little effect in the immediate neighbourhood. The castle chapel at Dover (c. 1181) is thus very similar in some of its details, and evidence has been found at Rochester that work of a like character was done after the fire there in 1179. Farther afield, however, its influence was not great, though it is perhaps to be recognized in the plan and certain other features of St. Hugh's church at Lincoln and also at Chichester.

The year of the completion of Canterbury saw also the burning of the church at Glastonbury and the beginning of the Lady Chapel there. Here the general lines and the ornament are definitely Romanesque throughout, except in the stone vault; the buttresses are of the flat pilaster type, but the vault was acutely pointed. In the great church, which was begun within a year or two after, a distinct advance was made, but this advance was on insular and not on French lines. The destruction of most of the building does not permit us to know how the main stone vaults of the church were supported, but the but-

---

[1] See Lasteyrie, *L'architecture . . . gothique*, i, p. 248.

PLATE 18

FOUNTAINS ABBEY, N. AISLE OF NAVE
c. 1140

STEYNING CHURCH (SUSSEX), NAVE
c. 1170–80

PLATE 19

WORKSOP PRIORY, NAVE
c. 1180

OXFORD CATHEDRAL, CHOIR
c. 1180 *with 16th century vault*

tresses are still only of Romanesque projection; all the arches, however, were pointed. The most unusual feature of the church is the internal elevation of the bays; here the main arches and a triforium passage with three openings are both included under a lofty wall-arch designed to give the effect of being the main arcade, partly filled in with the actual arch and the triforium above. The same idea carried out in a much more Romanesque form is to be seen at Oxford Cathedral (Pl. 19).[1] Here the arches throughout are round, and the actual arcades are sprung from the faces of the cylindrical piers which are carried up to support the wall-arches over the triforium. The date of this structure has been much disputed, but the character of its mouldings and decoration insist upon a period not earlier than 1170–80.[2] The nave of Worksop Priory (Pl. 19) must be later still, only here again the general effect is still Romanesque; the main arches are all round and the design of the interior is such as to render a stone vault impossible. The columns are alternately octagonal and round, and the large round arches of the triforium cut into and rise above the string-course at the base of the clearstory. This unusual arrangement compels the placing of the clearstory windows centrally above the main piers, and a small arch is placed below them and between the main arches of the triforium.

The round nave of the Temple Church, London (dedicated 1185), is structurally Gothic, though it has never had a stone vault over the main span. Its purely decorative features, however, like the intersecting wall-arcade and the great west doorway, are of traditional Romanesque form. The same juxtaposition in a single building is to be

---

[1] A tentative adoption of the same form is to be seen in the east bays of the nave at Romsey Abbey (Hants), and a third example, also of Romanesque form, may be cited in the presbytery of Jedburgh Abbey (Roxburghshire). See Macgibbon and Ross, *Ecclesiastical Architecture of Scotland*, i, p. 398.

[2] The completion of the building is probably indicated by the translation of the relics of St. Frideswide, which took place on 12 Feb. 1180. Digby MS. 177, p. 1, cited in *V.C.H., Oxford*, ii, p. 98.

seen in the nave of the Benedictine nunnery of Nun Monkton, where all the features are Gothic except the Romanesque west doorway, and Brinkburn Priory[1] is another example of a like nature.

With Archbishop Roger's church at Ripon (begun before 1180) we reach a structure which owes much to later Cistercian building. Many of the minor arches are round-headed, but the main arcades (except the crossing-arches) are pointed. The vaults were actually erected only over the aisles, and here occurs a new feature in the small rolls[2] which cover the pointed crowns of the vaulting-cells. There is an almost entire absence of Romanesque ornament.

The remaining great churches of the century little concern our purpose. Chichester choir, Wells Cathedral, and Lincoln Cathedral are Gothic structures in all their essential features, in which the bonds of Romanesque are only observable in minor points which are neither obtrusive nor important. Here and there a Romanesque detail lingered on into the thirteenth century, but for all practical purposes the close of the twelfth century saw the final eclipse of that tradition which had governed English architecture for so many centuries.

Minor Features. In minor structural features the second half of the twelfth century saw the introduction of a number of new forms and the final abandonment of certain old ones.

The form of the pier perhaps shows the greatest breaking away from the old traditions, for while the ordinary cylindrical and compound piers survived, beside them we find two new varieties. The first of these is formed by a greater or less complexity of grouped shafts not set against orders as in the compound pier but directly intersecting or touching one another. The simplest form of this device

---

[1] *Northumberland County History*, vii, p. 484.

[2] Cf. The earlier examples at Araines and Lucheux. C. Enlart, *Manuel* (2nd edit.), p. 490, n. 5.

produces the quatrefoil pier, such as may be seen in the nave of Tutbury Priory[1] (Staffs.), *c.* 1170, or Ramsey (Hunts.), *c.* 1180. Its more elaborate form was early introduced by the Cistercians, in the nave at Kirkstall, where the surfaces of the essentially cylindrical piers have a series of major and minor shafts worked upon them. Roche, Furness, and Byland show the grouping of the shafts which is typical of the full Gothic of the thirteenth century. Orford (Suffolk), and Ramsey (Hunts.) show examples of the cylindrical pier or shaft with small shafts or groups of shafts attached to its surface.

This brings us to the second variety of pier—the use of free-standing shafts either grouped round a central cylinder or themselves combining equally to support the superincumbent weight. There can be little doubt that the adoption of this form was very closely connected with the introduction of Purbeck or other marble as the material for free shafts, a fashion which had an extraordinary vogue in England during the thirteenth century. The main piers of the round nave of the Temple Church, London (*c.* 1185), consist of four equal-sized shafts of this material tied together by the capital and base and by a moulded band in the middle. The use of free shafts in conjunction with a cylindrical pier may be seen at Chichester choir (*c.* 1190), Selby Abbey, and elsewhere.

The necessity of a band-course to tie these free shafts together or to the main pier, when they are of any considerable length,[2] led also to its adoption as a decorative feature in instances where no structural need is apparent. It appears thus on the cylindrical piers of St. Peter's, Northampton (Pl. 7), and is often multiplied on the jamb-shafts of windows in the last quarter of the century. As applied to the free shafts of a doorway it sometimes appears in an

---

[1] *Brit. Arch. Assoc. Journ.*, vii, p. 390.
[2] Not only for reasons of stability but also because marble shafts were not obtainable above a certain length.

enlarged form, resembling the bezel of a seal, on the outward faces.

Two other minor features may here be noticed. The first is the change in the form of the abacus, which in the first two periods was almost invariably square in plan except when applied to large cylindrical piers such as Gloucester and Tewkesbury. The late period shows a frequent use of the octagonal abacus and beginnings of the use of the round form on all shafts whether large or small. This use is perhaps first seen in the crypt at Canterbury Cathedral (*c.* 1175) and became universal in thirteenth-century English work, in contradistinction to the French use which retained the square abacus throughout much of the thirteenth century.

The second feature is an alteration in form and even in function of the vaulting-rib. In the earlier periods this had formed a skeleton frame, structurally independent of the rubble vault which may or may not have settled down upon it. In the last phase the rib becomes an integral part of the vault, its voussoirs passing through the vault and being visible on the extrados. In this system the vault-web between the ribs is supported on a notch or rebate cut in the sides of the ribs themselves. The early adoption of this form of rib has been noted at Orford Castle (1166–7) and at Buildwas chapter-house (*c.* 1170), but it did not become general till an advanced date in the thirteenth century.

Chapter VI

ANGLO-NORMAN PARISH CHURCHES AND CHAPELS

SIDE by side with the rebuilding of the English cathedral and monastic churches after the Conquest, an almost equally extensive rebuilding of the parish churches took place throughout the country, though the process was probably spread over a much longer period and suffered a greater proportion of the earlier buildings to survive. Here and there, in the remoter parts of the country, the earlier methods and technique survived, likewise, and produced that hybrid type of building which is now generally referred to as the Saxo-Norman overlap. This type is most in evidence in Lincolnshire, which, by reason of a number of peculiarities of race, tenure, and customs, preserved a certain measure of isolation and impenetrability throughout the Middle Ages.

Elsewhere, the parish churches of the late eleventh and early twelfth centuries generally conform to a few standard types which in most cases are represented also in Normandy.

They display, however, a preponderance of the square east end, which represents a greater proportion than does the same feature, after the eleventh century, in the parish churches of Normandy. The geographical distribution of the known apsidal ends[1] in minor English churches shows that this form was far more frequent in the south-eastern part of the country, and may serve as some indication of the extent of the intensive penetration of the Norman masons into the rural districts. On the other hand a certain proportion of the square east ends may also be due to Norman masons, for this form itself was frequent in the early churches

---

[1] F. H. Fairweather, *Aisleless Apsidal Churches of Great Britain*, 1933.

of Normandy.[1] The very general adoption of the square end in the late Saxon period no doubt reinforced the latter influence, which was to oust almost entirely the apse from English practice, from about the middle of the twelfth century onwards. The subsequent very general destruction of apses, often to permit of the erection of large east windows for the display of stained glass, has rendered difficult any estimate of the original number of such features; their survival, furthermore, in groups in some parts of the country is no more evidence of a local fashion for building apses than for an almost equally local fashion for pulling them down.

In the smaller churches the proportions of the nave often approximate to two squares, that is to say the length is about double the width. This forms a useful distinction from the churches of the preceding late Saxon period, when the nave was commonly shorter in proportion to its width.

The aisleless churches of the late eleventh and the first half of the twelfth century group themselves into a number of types which will now be considered. These types have no geographical significance and though some differences are observable in the form of decoration adopted in the various districts, it is insufficient to form the basis of any classification.

(a) *Simple apartment type.* This is the simplest form, and is generally confined to buildings below the rank of parish church. The east end is either square or apsidal, but in neither case is there any structural division between the chancel and nave. Examples of the square-ended type may be seen at Harlowbury[2] (Essex) and Askham Bryan (Yorks.), and examples with the apsidal end at Little Tey (Fig. 33 h)[3] and Little Braxted[4] (Essex), Maplescombe[5] (Kent), Nately Scures[6] (Hants), &c.

---

[1] Examples, dating from the eleventh century, may be cited at Ouilly le Vicomte, S. Hippolyte de Canteloup, and S. Martin de la Lieue, all in Calvados.
[2] *Roy. Com. on Hist. Mons., Essex*, ii, p. 114.   [3] *Ibid.*, iii, p. 173.
[4] *Ibid.*, p. 162.   [5] *Brit. Arch. Ass. Journ.*, N.S., xxxiv, p. 225.
[6] *V.C.H., Hants*, iv, p. 154.

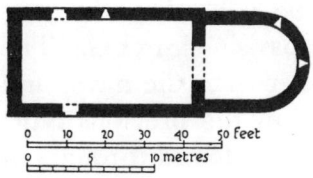

a. Bengeo. Herts.

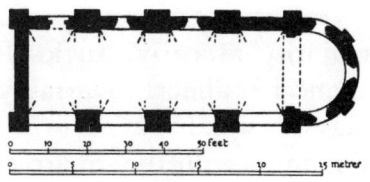

b. Copford. Essex.

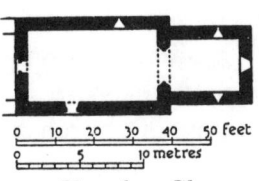

c. Kempley. Glos.

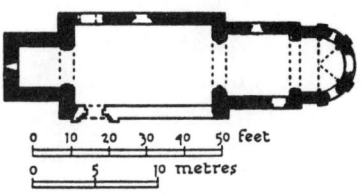

d. Birkin. Yorks.

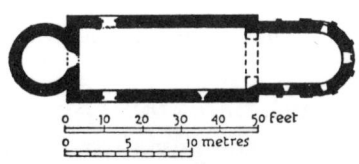

e. Hales. Norfolk.

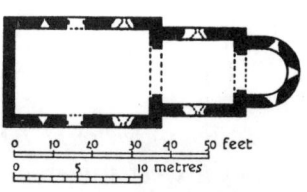

f. Moccas. Herefordshire.

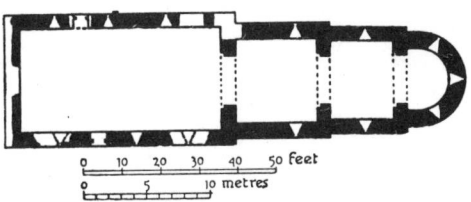

g. Peterchurch. Herefordshire.

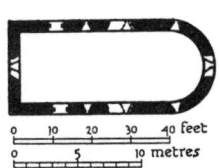

h. Little Tey. Essex.

FIG. 33. PARISH CHURCH PLANS.

(b) *Two-apartment type*. This type comprises the vast majority of early Anglo-Norman parish churches. The chancel is almost invariably narrower than the nave, and may be square-ended or apsidal as in the previous type. Examples with the square end are to be found throughout the country; the apsidal form is less common, but there are good instances at Bengeo[1] (Fig. 33 *a*) and Great Amwell (Herts.), Pentlow[2] and Hadleigh[3] (Essex), and a ruined one at Mells (Suffolk). As in the previous type the bells were hung in a bell-cote on the west gable.

(c) *Three-apartment type*. This type consists of a nave, square choir, and a square-ended or apsidal presbytery beyond it. The square choir often formed the base of a tower, but the commonest form of this type of church has only a bell-cote. The eastern compartment is commonly vaulted, with a semi-dome if an apse, and if a square, with a groined or ribbed vault. Examples with the apse are to be seen at Newhaven (Sussex), Steetley[4] (Derby), East Ham[5] (Essex), Kilpeck,[6] and Moccas[7] (Fig. 33 *f*) (Hereford), and with the square sanctuary at Colne St. Denis[8] (Glos.), Iffley[9] (Oxon.) before enlargement (Pl. 20), and Stewkley[10] (Bucks.).

(d) *Four-apartment type*. The usual form of this type includes a west tower in addition to the component parts of the previous type. There are examples (both with apses) at Great Maplestead[11] (Essex) and Birkin[12] (Fig. 33 *d*) (Yorks.). A more unusual four-apartment plan is that provided by Peterchurch[13] (Fig. 33 *g*) (Hereford); here the choir division

---

[1] *Arch. Journ.*, xliv, p. 26.
[2] *Roy. Com. on Hist. Mons., Essex*, i, p. 209.
[3] *Ibid.*, iv, p. 63.   [4] *Reliquary and Ill. Arch.*, N.S., xii, p. 73.
[5] *Roy. Com. on Hist. Mons., Essex*, ii, p. 59.
[6] *Ibid., Herefordshire*, i, p. 156.   [7] *Ibid.*, i, p. 204.
[8] Britton's *Archit. Antiquities*, v.
[9] *Brist. and Glos. Arch. Soc. Trans.*, l, p. 80.
[10] *Roy. Com. on Hist. Mons., Bucks.*, ii, p. 275.   [11] *Ibid., Essex*, i, p. 129.
[12] *Yorks. Arch. Soc. Excursion*, July 1897, p. 8.
[13] *Roy. Com. on Hist. Mons., Herefordshire*, i, p. 210.

PLATE 20

OZLEWORTH CHURCH (GLOUCESTERSHIRE)
TOWER
early 12th century

IFFLEY CHURCH, OXON
mid 12th century

PLATE 21

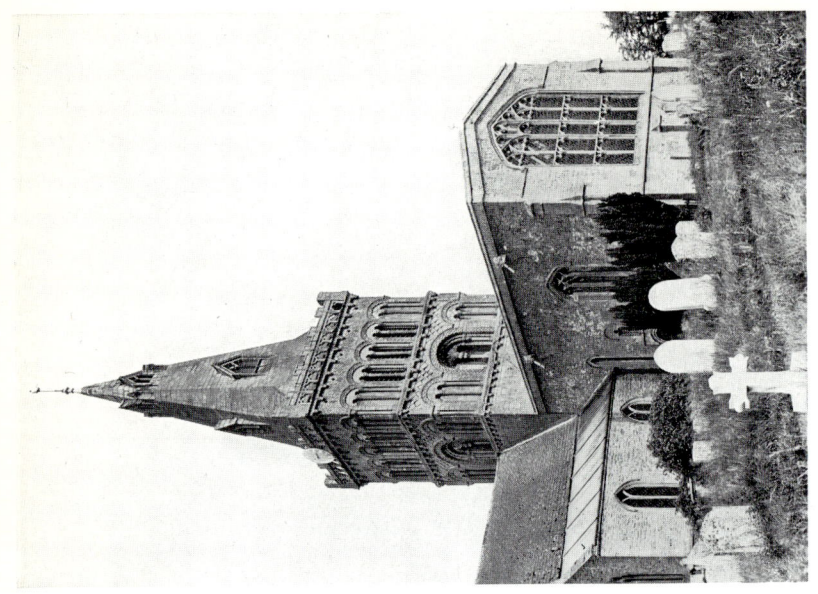

CASTOR, NORTHANTS, TOWER

c. 1124

SWAFFHAM PRIOR CHURCH
(CAMBS.) TOWER

c. 1150–80

is duplicated, the western compartment having once supported a tower.

(*e*) *The aisleless cruciform plan* with a central tower occurs in occasional instances throughout the country. Examples may be seen at Westham[1] and Old Shoreham[2] (Sussex), North Newbald[3] (Yorks.), Kingsclere[4] and East Meon[5] (Hants), Devizes, St. John (Wilts.), Stow[6] (Lincs.), and elsewhere. At Westham and Old Shoreham there is evidence of apsidal chapels, projecting east of the transept. Remains of a particularly valuable example (Pl. 21), as being definitely dated to the year 1124, exist at Castor[7] (Northants). Petersfield (Hants), originally aisleless, had a central tower with a second tower, added slightly later, at the west end.

(*f*) *Unusual types.* A few churches may be mentioned here which do not conform with any of the above types. In Kent and Sussex there is a small group of buildings each of which has a flanking tower on one side or other of the nave and provided with an eastern apse. This still exists at Godmersham but those at Bapchild and East Dean have been destroyed. A similar arrangement has been surmised at Kingsdown[8] and no doubt existed elsewhere.

The extraordinary tower at Fingest[9] (Bucks.), 27 ft. square externally, evidently served as the nave of the church, and may be compared to a few pre-Conquest towers which seem to have served a similar purpose, and with the two hexagonal towers in Gloucestershire, dealt with in Chapter VII.

Another isolated building is Compton church[10] (Surrey), where the chancel has an inserted lower story, both upper

---

[1] *Sussex Notes and Queries.*
[2] Plan by P. M. Johnston, in J. C. Cox, *The English Parish Church*, p. 100.
[3] *Yorks. Arch. Journ.*, xxi, p. 1.
[4] *V.C.H., Hants*, iv, p. 262.   [5] *Ibid.*, iii, p. 72.
[6] Partly of pre-Conquest date, *Ass. Archit. Soc. Rep.*, i, p. 315 (no plan).
[7] *V.C.H., Northants*, ii, p. 479.   [8] *Arch. Cant.*, xxxv, p. 3.
[9] *Roy. Com. on Hist. Mons., Bucks.*, i, p. 156.
[10] *V.C.H., Surrey*, iii, p. 22.

and lower chambers being open towards the west; the lower story has a stone vault.

The aisled parish churches of the period are generally confined to the smaller towns or large villages, and even here they hardly appear in the earlier part of the period. They are of two types: (*a*) cruciform with a central tower, or (*b*) chancel and aisled nave with or without a west tower.

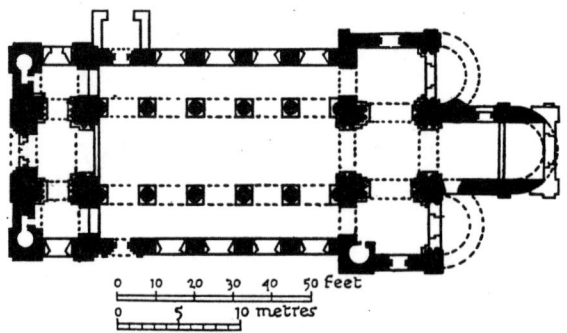

0   10   20   30   40   50 feet
0   5   10 metres

FIG. 34. Melbourne. Derby.

The cruciform type is that most common in the smaller towns. An almost complete example with a square east end is to be seen at Hemel Hempstead[1] (Herts.). Bishop's Cleeve[2] (Glos.) and Crondall[3] (Hants) may also be mentioned, and St. Chad's Stafford, is a richly ornamented but mutilated church of the same type. The finest example of this type, however, is the great church at Melbourne[4] (Fig. 34) (Derby), which had a central, and two western towers, apsidal chancel and apsidal chapels east of the transept, and an aisled nave (Pl. 22).

The second type, consisting of chancel and aisled nave, is commonly a development from one of the aisleless types, the aisles being added at a later date. In a number of instances, however, this plan was adopted when the church was built, as may be seen at Norham[5] (Northumberland)

[1] *Roy. Com. on Hist. Mons., Herts.*, p. 111.
[2] *Brist. and Glos. Arch. Soc. Trans.*, l, p. 82.
[3] *V.C.H., Hants*, iv, p. 11.   [4] *Arch.*, xiii, p. 290; *Arch. Journ.*, lxxi, p. 293.
[5] *Proc. Soc. Ant. Newcastle*, 2nd ser., v, p. 49, and 3rd ser., iii, p. 125 (no plan).

PLATE 22

ROCHESTER CATHEDRAL, NAVE
c. 1140–50

MELBOURNE CHURCH, DERBY, NAVE
c. 1140

PLATE 23

NORTHAMPTON, ST. SEPULCHRE
early 12th century (arches later)

and in later churches such as Northampton St. Peter,[1]
Castle Hedingham[2] (Essex), Ramsey[3] (Hunts.), &c. The
tower, while commonly placed at the west end, occasionally
stood between the chancel and nave as may be seen at
Great Tey[4] (Essex), though here the remarkable nave was
destroyed in 1829. In a few instances large churches of this
type were apparently unprovided with any tower; these are
generally to be found in immediate connexion with a monastic house, and the lack must be explained as an intentional
omission on the part of their monastic patrons.

The extension of aisles to part of the choir of a parish
church is a development of the latter part of the twelfth
century, and by the close of the century there are occasional
instances of aisles conterminous with the chancel itself.
Ledbury[5] (Hereford) may serve as an example of the par-
tially aisled choir, while New Shoreham[6] (Sussex) displays
the completed feature.

As we have seen, these larger parish churches are confined to the smaller towns, for the multiplication of churches
in the large towns, such as London, Norwich, York,
Winchester, and Canterbury, was such that little opportunity or excuse was afforded for the erection of any one
structure on a large scale. We have noted above the salient
features of the plan, but a few words may be added on the
other features of these buildings. The smaller churches
were entered by two doorways opposite one another and
towards the west end of the nave, the more important
structures having a west doorway in addition.

Vaulting was but sparingly used, and was generally
confined to the chancel. Kempley (Fig. 33 c) (Glos.), has a
barrel-vaulted chancel. Chancels with early groined vaults
survive at Colne St. Denis (Glos.) and elsewhere and there
are or were chancels with ribbed vaults at Devizes (St. John

[1] J. Britton, *Archit. Antiquities*, ii.
[2] *Roy. Com. on Hist. Mons., Essex*, i, p. 48.   [3] *Ibid., Hunts.*, p. 205.
[4] *Ibid., Essex*, iii, p. 130.   [5] *Ibid., Herefordshire*, ii, p. 101.
[6] E. Sharpe, *Arch. Hist. of St. Mary's Church, New Shoreham.*

and St. Mary), Hemel Hempstead (Herts.), Gloucester (St. Mary de Lode), Slough (Bucks.), Rudford (Glos.), Warkworth (Northumberland), and various other places. The internal elevation of the aisled churches is normally provided with a clearstory of round or round-headed windows, and very occasionally, as at Melbourne, the clearstory has a continuous wall-passage. The towers[1] often exhibit considerable elaboration, both externally as at Castor (Pl. 21) (Northants), Sandwich St. Clement, Dover St. Mary, Leicester St. Nicholas, or internally as at Devizes St. John's, or Petersfield. This elaboration commonly takes the form of interlacing arcading, and the example at Devizes[2] is remarkable as perhaps the only instance, in this country, of a triple interlacing, that is to say with the arches sprung over three intervening bays. The west front is sometimes also enriched with arcading as at Castle Rising[3] (Norfolk). Porches are not a common adjunct in parish churches of this age, but occasionally exist in the larger examples.[4] A more common feature was to set the doorway in a projection or thickening of the wall, finished with a gable; of this there are fine examples at Patrixbourne and St. Margaret at Cliffe (Kent), Adel, Kilham, and Newbald (Yorks.), and a group in Worcestershire[5] with arcading above the doorway.

Carved decoration in parish churches will be dealt with in the chapter dealing with ornament. Curiously enough it occurs in its greatest profusion in some of the smallest churches; such well-known examples as Barfreston[6] (Kent), Kilpeck (Hereford), Studland[7] (Dorset), and Tickencote (Pl. 29) (Rutland) are cases in point.

[1] A west tower of unusual form survives at Swaffham Prior (Cambridgeshire). Here (Pl. 21) the ground stage is square, the second stage octagonal, and the superstructure sixteen-sided.   [2] J. Britton, *Archit. Antiquities*, ii.
[3] H. Bowman, *Specimens of Ancient Eccl. Architecture*, 1846.
[4] E.g. Breedon (Worcs.).
[5] At Bockleton, Knighton-on-the-Teme, Stoulton, and Easham.
[6] *Archit. Ass. Sketch Book*, 1867–8 and 1890; J. Britton, *Archit. Antiquities*, iv.
[7] *Brit. Arch. Ass. Journ.*, N.S., xxiv, p. 35.

Chapter VII

CENTRALLY PLANNED CHURCHES

THE centrally planned type of building, in England, is largely confined to those structures modelled on the form of the Church of the Holy Sepulchre at Jerusalem, a form which received a remarkable impetus as a result of the early Crusades. The round church was early adopted by the military orders of the Temple and the Hospital of St. John of Jerusalem, but was by no means confined to their ranks. There seems little doubt that every twelfth-century church bearing the dedication of St. Sepulchre was originally built in this form, and in addition to this there are three or four known instances of round churches with other dedications and connected with neither of the military orders.

The five surviving round churches in England are those of St. Sepulchre Cambridge, St. Mary Magdalene in Ludlow Castle, St. Sepulchre Northampton, the Temple Church London, and the much later (fourteenth-century) church of the Hospitallers at Little Maplestead. Other examples, now destroyed, have been discovered by excavation or are evidenced by documentary sources. The form is so unusual in England that a complete list may be given here with the approximate dates and connexions.[1]

---

[1] A general account of most of these churches with plans is given by Sir W. H. St. J. Hope in *Rep. of Chap. Gen.*, St. John of Jerusalem, 1916, p. 6. For the New Temple, London, see *Roy. Com. on Hist. Mons., London*, iv, p. 138; Temple Bruer, *Arch.*, lxi, p. 177; Garway, *Antiq. Journ.*, viii, p. 238; Clerkenwell, *Roy. Com. on Hist. Mons., London*, ii, p. 17; Little Maplestead, *Roy. Com. on Hist. Mons., Essex*, i, p. 184; Cambridge, J. Britton, *Archit. Antiquities*, i; Northampton, *Ibid.*, i; Ludlow, *Arch.*, lxi, p. 271; Hereford, St. Giles, *Roy. Com. on Hist. Mons., Hereford*, i, p. 131; W. Thurrock, *Essex Arch. Soc. Trans.*, N.S., xiii, p. 53.

Templar.	*Hospitaller.*
Old Temple, London, *c.* 1135.	Clerkenwell, London, *c.* 1140.
New Temple, London, 1186.	Little Maplestead, fourteenth century.
Temple Bruer, twelfth century.	
Garway, late twelfth century.	*Parish Churches.*
Bristol Temple.	Cambridge, early twelfth century.
Aslakeby Temple.	Northampton, early twelfth century.
Dover, twelfth century.	West Thurrock, early twelfth century.
Private Chapels.	*Hospital-chapel.*
Ludlow Castle, early twelfth century.	Hereford, St. Giles, mid-twelfth cen-
Woodstock Palace.	tury.

The larger type of these buildings had an inner arcade of
six, or more commonly eight, bays, supporting, at the New

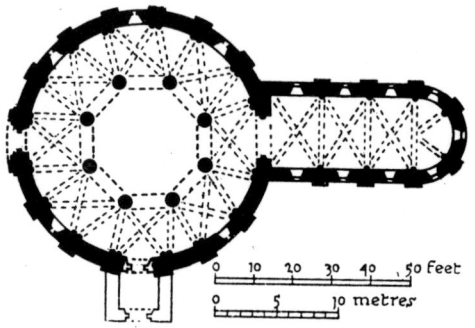

Fig. 35. St. Sepulchre. Northampton.

Temple, London, and at St. Sepulchre, Cambridge, a
triforium and clearstory. The chancel in all these churches
was originally aisleless, and either apsidal or square-ended.
St. Sepulchre's at Northampton (Fig. 35 and Pl. 23) retains
only its outer circular wall and colonnade; the aisle appears
to have been vaulted in stone, a feature which soon forced
the circular wall outwards and necessitated the removal of
the vault and the rebuilding of the arcade in a pointed
form in the thirteenth century.

The smaller type, represented by the still existing chapel
at Ludlow (Fig. 36), had no internal arcade, but was carried
up to a considerable height. The destroyed churches at West
Thurrock (Essex), the temple church on the western heights
at Dover, and the chapel of St. Giles's Hospital at Hereford

were also buildings of this type, but the last-named is peculiar in that it appears to have had a small eastern apse
springing directly from the round nave in a manner similar
to that of the little ruined chapel of Orphir in the Orkney
Isles.

The Hospitaller church at Clerkenwell has, and the
church at Temple Bruer had, a crypt under the chancel,

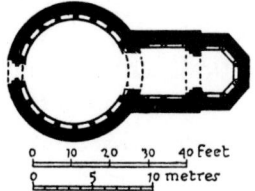

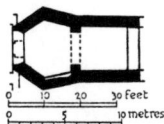

FIG. 36. Ludlow Castle. Chapel.   FIG. 37. Ozleworth. Glos.

and both were extended eastwards late in the twelfth century.

A somewhat cognate type of building is represented by the
two Gloucestershire village churches of Ozleworth (Fig. 37)[1]
and Swindon. Both these structures include early twelfth-
century towers of a remarkable irregular hexagonal form.
The side towards the east is considerably longer than the
others, and contains a wide arch. At Ozleworth (Pl. 20) this
opened into a chancel which seems to have completed the
building, the hexagonal tower thus doing duty as the nave.
At Swindon, however, there are both nave and chancel east
of the tower, and though the former has been rebuilt the
chancel retains traces of twelfth-century work. It seems
useless to speculate on the origin of this remarkable pair
of buildings which occupies a position equally isolated in
English or continental Romanesque. The detail of the
tower-windows at Ozleworth is of early form and exhibits
the simple volute-capital of the Norman type.

Lastly some consideration must be given to a still more
uncommon type of building of which only one example is

[1] T. Overbury in *Brist. and Glos. Arch. Soc. Trans.*, xliii, p. 360.

known to have existed in this country. William of Malmesbury[1] records that Robert of Lorraine, Bishop of Hereford (1079–95), built there a church after the fashion of Charlemagne's minster at Aachen. If by this he meant to imply a round or polygonal building, no trace of any such remains. There does, however, exist part of a remarkable chapel[2] (Fig. 38) of late eleventh-century date which was mostly destroyed in the first half of the eighteenth century. Drawings[3] were, however, made before

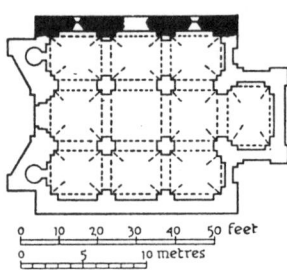

FIG. 38. Hereford. Bishop's Chapel.

its destruction, which show that it was a square building of two stories with four central columns supporting a clearstory and a square chancel to the east. It formed the chapel of the Bishop's palace and as such takes its place naturally in a group of kindred structures to be found in the Rhineland and north-eastern France, a district including the native place of its builder. The episcopal palaces at Laon and Mainz still retain precisely similar structures as do or did the castles of Eger, Nuremberg, Schwartz-Rheindorf, and others.[4] All these, curiously enough, appear to be of later date than the Hereford example. Called in Germany *Doppel-Kapellen*, they consisted of two stories, of which the upper one formed a gallery round the open central space which was carried up as a clearstory. Charlemagne's palace-chapel at Aachen is constructed on a similar scheme, though here the whole structure is polygonal. It is thus likely that Bishop Robert's structure at Hereford is the one referred to by William of Malmesbury.

---

[1] *Gesta Pont.* (Rolls Ser.), p. 300.
[2] *Roy. Com. on Hist. Mons., Hereford*, i, p. 115.
[3] *Vetusta Monumenta*, i, Pl. 49.
[4] See plans of Laon in *Cong. Arch. de France*, (Reims) 1912, i, p. 220; Mainz in *Cong. Arch. de France* (1924), p. 171; and for Eger see W. Lübke, *Geschichte der Architektur*, p. 342.

Chapter VIII

MASONRY AND MOULDINGS

MATERIALS and *Masonry*. The materials used by the Anglo-Norman builders depended, of course, primarily on the presence or absence of suitable building-stone in the immediate neighbourhood. Various parts of England produce stone of admirable quality for this purpose, and of these, the district round Peterborough, including Ketton, Barnack, and Ancaster; South Yorkshire, including Tadcaster, Huddlestone and Roche Abbey; Somersetshire, including Bath, Doulting, and Ham Hill, are the most important centres. Other parts of England possess stone of inferior quality or durability, such as the red sandstones of Chester, the Midlands, and Hereford, while still other districts provide a stone which cannot be worked, and is only useful for rubble walling. Most of these quarries were used locally throughout the period, and a few such as Barnack and the Somerset oolites were of such excellence as to be in demand at considerable distances. Thus Barnack stone was in use throughout the eastern and south-eastern counties from an early date in the twelfth century, and Bath stone was much used in South Wales and was even transported, after the English conquest, into Ireland.

In the districts where building-stone was of poor quality or non-existent, such as East Anglia and the Home counties, it was necessary, in the greater churches, to make use of non-local materials. It is true that the surviving remains of the Confessor's church at Westminster are built entirely of the easily worked but very soft firestone from Reigate (Surrey), but this material was not considered sufficiently durable by the Anglo-Norman builders, and it hardly again makes its appearance in the larger buildings until the latter part of the twelfth century, and then only for internal work. In its place the Norman builders of the south-eastern counties, and occasionally farther afield, imported Caen stone from Normandy, which forms the staple freestone of all the great churches of this part of England until in part supplanted by Barnack stone early in the twelfth century.

Though lacking in actual freestone of sufficient quality, south-east England supplied a variety of materials sufficiently good for rubble walling and rough work. Calcareous tufa, a lime deposit found in restricted areas in various parts of the country (e.g. Kent and Herefordshire), was a material both extremely light in weight, and easy to work.[1] It was extensively used by the Romans, and much of the tufa used in early Anglo-Norman buildings is re-used Roman material. The supply, in the south-east, seems to have been exhausted by or soon after the end of the eleventh century, and its employment in this part of England is thus some evidence for an early date. In other parts, however, the use of local tufa continued well on into the twelfth century.[2] Other Roman materials, such as bricks and septaria or hardened clay, were also re-used in the south-east during the same period, wherever a ruined Roman building supplied a quarry. Thus St. Albans Abbey was built in great part of Roman bricks from Verulamium, but throughout the district the supply seems to have come to an end by about the middle of the twelfth century.

The chalk counties provided an inexhaustible supply of flint, and this was used throughout East Anglia for rubble cores even in some of the largest churches.

Flint, when used on the face of a wall, is commonly, in the eleventh and twelfth centuries, carefully coursed, and the individual flints are pitched slightly on the rake so as

[1] Tufa in large blocks is used very freely in the eleventh-century east range of Westminster Abbey, and in a large number of buildings throughout Kent and Essex.

[2] As in the twelfth-century church of Moccas Herefordshire, which is built almost entirely of this material.

to give a vague impression of herring-bone work. The true herring-bone work[1] is always executed in rubble, and is most marked where stone split in comparatively shallow layers is used. It generally occurs sporadically in a wall, in occasional courses or patches, and seems to have been introduced with the idea of strengthening the construction, though it is difficult to see in the majority of cases what advantage was gained. It is practically always an indication of early date, and though it was used occasionally in the Saxon period it is commonly distinctive of late eleventh-century building. Good examples can be seen in a group of churches round Bulmer[2] (Yorks.), at Egremont Castle (Cumberland), at Bampton (Oxon.), at Bredwardine, Edvin Loach,[3] and Wigmore (Hereford), and at Ashleworth[4] (Glos.). At Tamworth Castle the curtain-wall, climbing up the steep slope of the keep-mound, is built almost entirely in this manner, and an early building at Corfe Castle is similarly constructed. Occasionally the herring-bone courses, as at Tamworth, are separated by a layer or course of flat stones, and still more occasionally the individual stones of the herring-bone were cut to fit their positions. This may be seen in the masonry-skin added to the Saxon wall of the nave at Diddlebury[5] (Salop).

Rubble walling, in the smaller churches, preserved a fairly constant thickness of about 3 ft., which was only increased when a stone vault was intended or when the height or scale of the building was above the normal. Walls of this type seem to have been invariably plastered and lime-washed both inside and out; even the Roman brick-work at St. Albans was so treated,[6] as were the external

---

[1] *Cumberland and Westmorland Arch. Soc. Trans.*, xxviii, p. 142.
[2] *V.C.H., N. Riding*, iii, p. 111; compare Terrington, *ibid.*, p. 205.
[3] *Roy. Com. on Hist. Mon., Hereford*, i, p. 25; ii, p. 75.
[4] *Brist. and Glos. Arch. Soc. Trans.*, xliii, p. 379.
[5] Baldwin Brown, *The Arts in Early England. Architecture* (2nd edit.), p. 245.
[6] Mathew Paris, *Vita Viginti Trium Sti. Albani Abbatum* (ed. W. Wats), 1684, p. 1016.

wall-faces of the White Tower, Tower of London in 1241.[1]

Anglo-Norman ashlar was commonly employed in blocks rather under a foot square, probably a size originally determined by convenience of carriage and subsequently adopted as a building-convention where little or no carriage was necessary. The exposed surface, throughout the period, was axed or tooled to a fair face by diagonal lines, coarsely executed in the earlier period but more finely worked through the twelfth century, according to the tool employed. This diagonal tooling was superseded, except in occasional instances,[2] round about the year 1200 by a tooling of vertical lines, and this general abandonment, at an almost even date throughout the country, is a very useful indication of period.

Late eleventh-century masonry is distinguished also by the thickness of its mortar joints, a practice which gave way to fine-jointed work early in the twelfth century and was sufficiently noticeable to attract the attention of William of Malmesbury who records[3] its adoption by Roger, Bishop of Sarum (1107–42): 'He erected extensive buildings . . . the courses of stone being so correctly laid that the joint deceives the eye and leads it to imagine that the whole wall is composed of a single block.'[4]

Occasionally, from the eleventh century onwards, when a square head is used to support the tympanum of an arch, the lintel is made up of several stones joggled together, that is to say with the joints cut and fitted together with a rebated or zigzag joint. A primitive example may be seen at Hatfield (Herefordshire), and a much later one at Orford Castle.

---

[1] Liberate Roll 25, Hen. iii, m. 20, cited in J. Bayley, *Tower of London*, 1830, i, p. 102.

[2] E.g. Wells Cathedral (undercroft of chapter-house).

[3] *Gesta Regum* (Rolls Ser.), ii, p. 484.

[4] An example of Bishop Roger's fine-jointed masonry is to be seen in the castle at Sherborne (Dorset).

The decorative treatment of ashlar wall-surfaces, though of occasional occurrence in Normandy[1] (e.g. S. Taurin, Evreux, south transept), hardly appears in England except in small surfaces such as tympana and gables where the stones form a diagonal or square chequer-pattern. In the monastic buildings at Westminster, however, there are two instances of such a treatment of a plain wall-surface—at the end of the frater-range, and on one face of the rere-dorter; both appear to date from the end of the eleventh century. Polychrome ornament produced by the alternation of two or more different coloured stones is likewise very little used in English work; the alternation of Northamptonshire ironstone and oolite is, however, sparingly used in that part of the country, and a similar practice has been noticed in the remains of the twelfth-century nave at Exeter, in Worcester chapter-house, and elsewhere. The painted reproduction on the great crossing arches of St. Albans Abbey show that its decorative use was both known and approved.

Foundations. Early Anglo-Norman building varied remarkably in its structural stability, for while the principles of secure foundation were evidently understood, their application was often neglected. Thus in many instances the foundations, construction, and the quality of the mortar are alike excellent, in others all three are equally faulty, the builders relying rather on thickness of wall than on stability of foundation. The use of ashlar as a facing to a rubble core necessitates the use of good mortar to give it any sort of cohesion, and Norman mortar was of very varying quality. From faults of this nature resulted the collapse of many early towers or other important parts of the building, which are recorded from time to time by the annalists.

On the other hand many buildings display the greatest

[1] A single instance of the V-shaped tailing together of the voussoirs of an arch of two rings, common in central France, occurs in the chancel-arch of Manningford Bruce (Wilts.).

care in their foundations. The apse at Durham, for instance, had foundations, in part at any rate, 14 ft. deep carried down to the rock, and the main structures at Westminster Abbey and Ely, owing to the nature of the site, were built on an elaborate system of sleeper-walls carried along under the main arcades. It was also a common practice to carry sleeper-walls across the chords of the apses of the earlier Anglo-Norman buildings.

As a further method of strengthening foundations on a site of doubtful stability, the Anglo-Normans resorted to the very ancient system of bond-timbers. An elaborate system of this nature was used by the Romans at Pevensey and elsewhere, and a similar elaborate construction has been found in the foundations of the early church at York, tentatively associated with the ninth-century building of Archbishop Albert. The Normans probably used it far more frequently than we suspect, for it is only occasionally that the destruction of a wall to the right level enables the evidence of this construction to become apparent. When used in foundations it appears to have consisted of timbers properly framed together and laid flat so as to be entirely enveloped in the masonry. The continuation of this system throughout the foundation undoubtedly tended to strengthen it so long as the timbers survived. Traces of such bond-timbers have been found in the eleventh-century curtain-wall at Richmond Castle,[1] under angle-turrets at Goodrich and Clifford Castles, and a rather different system has left extensive traces in the ruins of the dorter and rere-dorter at Lewes Priory. Here the holes left by the timbers, often a foot or more square, are at a higher level, and ran in the thickness of the wall completely round the building and were tied across it at intervals.

Mouldings. The principal mouldings, which serve as dating evidence in eleventh and twelfth-century English buildings, may be dealt with under the following heads:

---

[1] *Report of the Inspector of Ancient Monuments,* 1913, p. 24.

(*a*) base-mouldings; (*b*) abaci; (*c*) arch-mouldings; and (*d*) vaulting-ribs.

Base-mouldings (Fig. 39). Except in the very early period (late eleventh century), when certain erratic examples occur, the base-moulding follows a well-defined process of development which, though an absolute equation in date is not to

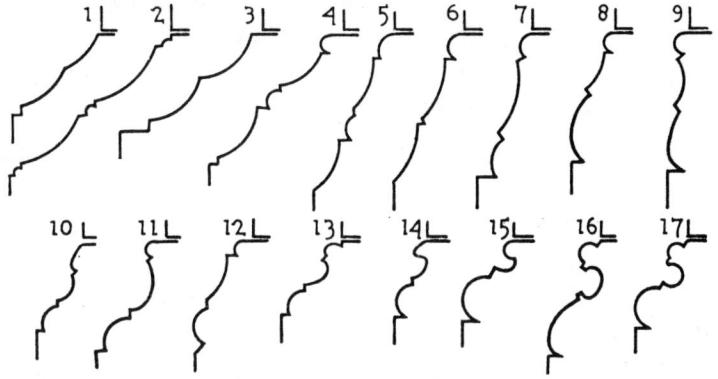

FIG. 39. Base Mouldings.

1. Westminster Abbey Choir, *c.* 1050. 2. Winchester Chapter-house, late 11th century. 3. Chester St. John's Crossing, *c.* 1140. 4. Winchester Crypt, *c.* 1075. 5, 6. Gloucester Choir Triforium, late 11th century. 7. Chichester Choir, *c.* 1100. 8. Norwich Choir, *c.* 1100. 9. Bath Crossing, *c.* 1110. 10. Durham Castle Chapel, *c.* 1072. 11, 12. Canterbury Cathedral, 1st Extension, *c.* 1110–20. 13. Lewes Priory SW. Tower, *c.* 1140. 14. Orford Castle, *c.* 1166–7. 15. Newcastle Castle Chapel, *c.* 1172–7. 16. Lesnes Abbey, *c.* 1180. 17. Dover Castle Chapel, *c.* 1181–8.

be expected, was yet very general throughout the country. The early examples are commonly distinguished by a very shallow cutting which, as time went on, was gradually deepened and the members accentuated until the maximum depth of cutting was achieved in the thirteenth century.

The double hollow-chamfer was a common Norman form of base, and was introduced into England in the Confessor's church at Westminster (*c.* 1050). It may be seen also in other early churches such as St. Augustine's, Canterbury (*c.* 1080), and Durham choir (*c.* 1095), and though commonly an indication of early date appears to have lingered on in such buildings as Hexham Priory nave (*c.* 1120), Chester Cathedral (north-west tower *c.* 1130), and Chester St. John's (choir *c.* 1130–40).

The crude attic base, seen occasionally in the early Normandy churches, appears first in England at Durham Castle chapel (1072), and from that point seems to have developed in two parallel lines, both shallow-cut, but the one preserving an almost vertical plane and the other with a great projection. The first may be seen at Bath Abbey (crossing *c.* 1100), Hereford Cathedral (*c.* 1115), &c., and the second at Canterbury Cathedral (crypt *c.* 1100 and Conrad's choir *c.* 1110–20). This second type of the moulding, consisting of a small roll divided by a shallow hollow from a large roll below, can be traced in its gradual deepening and development through the first half of the twelfth century. At first sight it would appear to be the original from which was developed the typical hold-water base of the last third of the century, but the immediate links between the two seem to be lacking and it is more probable that the developed hold-water base was an introduction from France after the middle of the twelfth century. The addition or accentuation of its individual members can be closely dated as may be seen by the accompanying series of examples. The slightly flattened lower roll introduced in some Cistercian churches and in the second extension at Canterbury (*c.* 1170–80) was soon abandoned for the rounded form.

Other forms of base-moulding make an occasional appearance but have little significance. Such are the single roll at Winchester (choir *c.* 1080–5), the hollow with two rolls below at Blyth Priory (*c.* 1080–90), and the accumulation of small members found on some of the bases of the first extension at Canterbury (*c.* 1100–30). The occasional occurrence of a bulbous form of base derived from an Anglo-Saxon original may also be noted. The base-moulding of a round column or shaft always rested

on a square plinth, except in a few occasional instances of
cylindrical columns of exceptionally large diameter.

Abaci and *String-courses* (Fig. 40). With the exception of the
necking, the abacus of an eleventh or twelfth-century capital
is commonly the only part of it which is actually moulded.
In one early example (Westminster, dorter sub-vault *c.*
1070) the abacus forms a square slab with a chamfer below

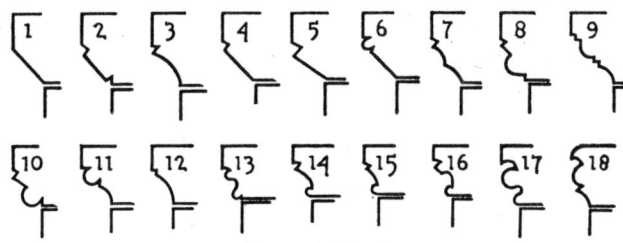

FIG. 40. Abaci.

1. General, 11th–12th century. 2. Ely, *c.* 1080. 3. Winchester Crypt, *c.* 1080.
4. Peterborough, *c.* 1120. 5. Southwell, *c.* 1108. 6. Wimborne, *c.* 1160–70. 7–9.
Elstow, *c.* 1150. 10. Orford Castle, *c.* 1166. 11. Ely Infirmary, *c.* 1160. 12.
Fountains, *c.* 1135, and Kirkstall, *c.* 1152. 13. Malmesbury, *c.* 1160. 14. Roche,
c. 1175. 15. Canterbury, *c.* 1177–8. 16. Chichester Choir, *c.* 1190. 17. New
Shoreham, *c.* 1190. 18. Steyning, *c.* 1170.

it following the curve of the column, and at Durham Castle
chapel, the abacus has a large roll.

In general the abaci are of square section with a cham-
fered under-edge. Very soon, however, this was relieved
by a nick or groove above and sometimes also below the
chamfer (e.g. Ely *c.* 1080, Norwich *c.* 1100, Peterborough
c. 1120, &c.). This form remained long unaltered. The
next step was to hollow the chamfer and this appears early
at Winchester and later at Fountains (*c.* 1140), Kirkstall
(*c.* 1155), and in numerous other places. In the second
half of the century a variety of mouldings were introduced in which the original outline was soon entirely lost.
Examples of these later varieties may be seen at Orford
Castle (1166), Malmesbury (*c.* 1165), Canterbury Cathedral
(1174–84), Ely Infirmary (*c.* 1160), New Shoreham, and
Chichester choir (*c.* 1190).

The impost mouldings of square piers, without shafts, occasionally show a greater variety than the earlier abaci. This is exemplified at Elstow Abbey nave which may perhaps date from the first half of the twelfth century.

Abacus-mouldings were repeated unaltered in string-courses and labels of the same age, the only variation being the occasional chamfering of the upper edge of the string in addition to the lower edge.

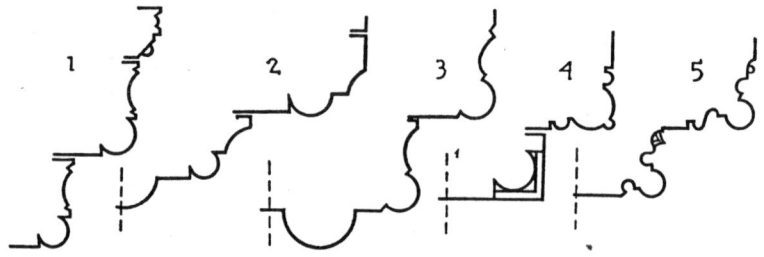

FIG. 41. Arch-mouldings.

1. Caen S. Étienne W. Doorway, *c.* 1080. 2. Durham Choir arcade, *c.* 1095. 3. Chester St. John's Choir arcade, *c.* 1140. 4. Orford (Suffolk) Choir arcade, *c.* 1166. 5. Canterbury Choir arcade, *c.* 1175–80.

Arch-mouldings (Fig.41). The arch-mouldings of the earlier Anglo-Norman churches are confined to rolls projecting from the soffits of the orders. They differ from the common twelfth-century form of roll-moulding in that they are not set symmetrically in the angle of the orders but indicate by their plan the direction in which the arch springs. Winchester, Ely, and Durham provide examples of this arrangement. In the last instance, Durham choir (*c.* 1095), the angles of the arch-orders are further enriched by rolls and hollow-chamfers. In the smaller arches, such as doorways and triforium arches,[1] a further elaboration was adopted by the cutting of a shallow hollow on the face of the order, combined with a roll on its angle. In the early examples these mouldings are closely compressed into the square outline of the order, but in the twelfth century they acquire

[1] E.g. Norwich presbytery.

more freedom and depth of cutting. The same form was
adopted for the orders of the main arcade as at St. John's,
Chester (*c.* 1140), and prepared the way for the more
elaborate mouldings of the orders of the arch.

A definite advance is marked by the reduction of the
angle-rolls to quite small dimensions and the addition of

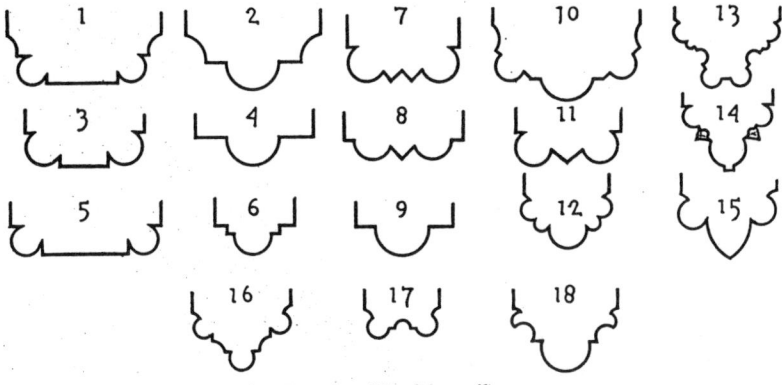

FIG. 42. Vaulting-ribs.

1. Durham Choir aisle cross-arch, *c.* 1095. 2. Durham Choir aisle rib, *c.* 1095.
3. Peterborough Choir aisle cross-arch, *c.* 1120. 4. Peterborough Choir aisle
rib, *c.* 1120. 5. Lindisfarne Priory Nave cross-arch, *c.* 1120. 6. Canterbury
Treasury rib, *c.* 1150. 7. Southwell Nave rib, *c.* 1130. 8. Selby Nave cross-arch,
c. 1150. 9. Selby Nave rib, *c.* 1150. 10. Romsey Nave S. aisle rib, *c.* 1140.
11. Peterborough Nave cross-arch, *c.* 1150. 12. Malmesbury Nave rib, *c.* 1160–5.
13. Canterbury Choir cross-arch, *c.* 1177–8. 14. Canterbury Choir rib, *c.* 1177–8.
15. St. Cross Choir rib, *c.* 1160–70. 16. Glastonbury Lady Chapel cross-arch,
c. 1186. 17. Glastonbury Lady Chapel rib, *c.* 1186. 18. Oxford Cathedral
Choir rib, *c.* 1170–80.

subsidiary rolls flanking the hollows; the result is a moulding
which, while still restrained within the square lines of the
order from which it is cut, has already most of the features
of the full Gothic moulding. This advance appears in
William of Sens's work at Canterbury, and may subsequently be seen at Dover Castle chapel (1181–8), Rochester
(fragments after the fire of 1179), New Shoreham (*c.* 1190),
and finally still more elaborated at Wells (*c.* 1195). In the
last two instances some of the rolls are brought to a point
or edge.

Vaulting-ribs (Fig. 42). Vaulting-ribs are of two kinds, those forming the main cross-arches (*doubleaux*) between the bays, and the diagonal ribs (*ogives*) reinforcing the groins of the vaults. The cross-arches are nearly always present in early groined vaulting and are then of plain square section. Ribs of this form also occur occasionally in ribbed vaults but are very exceptional in this connexion.[1] The ordinary early form of rib in England consists of a half-roll applied to the soffit of a rib, with square or hollow-chamfered angles. This is the form adopted at Durham choir (*c.* 1095), Peterborough choir (*c.* 1120), Winchester transept (*c.* 1120), Romsey choir (*c.* 1125), Devizes, St. John and St. Mary (*c.* 1130–40), &c. The cross-arches, accompanying these ribs, have two either soffit or angle-rolls divided by either a plain surface or a pointed member. Later ribs are often provided with two subsidiary rolls either set on the angle of the order or grouped with the main roll.

Later twelfth-century ribs exhibit the same process of elaboration and deepening of mouldings as the arch-mouldings, and here again the bringing to a point of some of the rolls is observable. This stage is best exemplified at Durham Chapter-house (1133–40), St. Cross, Winchester (*c.* 1160–70), Canterbury (William of Sens's work, 1176–8), and Glastonbury (Lady Chapel, *c.* 1186). In the last three cases some of the ribs are enriched with cheveron-ornament.

---

[1] Warwick crypt, Berkswell crypt, Beaudesert choir.

Chapter IX

ORNAMENT AND SCULPTURE

ANGLO-NORMAN building of the eleventh century is remarkable for its almost entire lack of ornament of any description. In the surviving early parts of Winchester, Gloucester, Worcester, and other great churches it would be difficult to find any serious attempt to relieve the severity of the plain cubical or cushion-capitals or the bare simplicity of the other features. The Normans, it is true, brought with them the billet-ornament, the plain diaper, and the simple volute capital. This last appears in such places as St. John's chapel in the Tower of London, the chapel (Pl. 11) in Durham Castle, the west front at Lincoln, and not uncommonly elsewhere in England. In the few instances where a more elaborate decoration is attempted it only bears evidence to the entire inability of the Norman mason of that age to carve effectively in stone. One of the capitals[1] in the castle chapel at Durham is carved with human figures of such crude and barbarous deformity as to indicate only too well the stage of advancement in this art arrived at by masons, working on one of the most important buidings in the north.

It is not difficult to say at what precise period this poverty of ornament began to give place to the introduction of that florid enrichment which was to distinguish the later phases of Anglo-Norman romanesque. We shall see that the cheveron ornament led the way in the gradual enrichment of the arch-mouldings, being introduced about 1110–20. It was followed very shortly by all the other forms of enrichment; the minster at Southwell built about 1115–30 is still comparatively restrained in all its features, and indeed exhibits hardly any other ornament than the cheveron and cable

[1] G. Baldwin Brown in *Antiquity*, v, p. 438.

ornament in its architecture.[1] Between this date and the middle of the century nearly all the other forms had been introduced, and one of the richest and most elaborate examples of Anglo-Norman romanesque, at Shobdon (Hereford), was finished before the death of Bishop Robert de Bethune in 1148.[2] We may thus confine the rise of this romanesque ornament to the period 1110–50. To the same period belongs the introduction and development of the sculptured capital, if indeed it is not of slightly earlier date. It is, however, always difficult to be certain if the carving on a capital is contemporary with the structure on which it is carved, unless the position is so inaccessible as to render the addition of carving an unlikely and too costly performance. This, for instance, may be said to apply to the carving of the capitals on the crossing at Southwell, which must thus date from about 1120–5. Earlier than these are perhaps the capitals of the east presbytery-arch at Hereford, built about 1115, and the detached capitals said to have come from Westminster Hall, built about 1090–1100. In both these cases, however, the carving may easily have been added later, and none of the capitals remaining in situ at Westminster Hall exhibits any enrichment whatsoever.

The true Anglo-Norman romanesque foliage of the first half of the twelfth century is almost entirely of acanthus-type. It differs, however, from the elaborate acanthus-scrolls of the Anglo-Saxon Winchester school not only by its more substantial structure but also by the introduction of a distinctive form of stem, consisting of a row of pellets flanked by plain bands or strands, by the introduction or accentuation of the moulded bands at the branch-junctions, and finally by the freer use of beast-heads from which, occasionally, the branches emerge. This foliage is seldom used as an architectural feature, being confined, in stone, to such minor surfaces as fonts (Pl. 43) and tympana.

[1] There is a simple beak-head on the innermost order of the north doorway.
[2] Dugdale, *Mon. Ang.* (1830), vi, p. 345.

Side by side with this development of purely continental romanesque, there appears to have subsisted a parallel art which seems to owe its origins to the native carving of the previous age. It is largely confined to village churches and can thus be hardly ever exactly dated, but is often found in juxtaposition to purely Norman architectural forms. Its distinguishing features are the use of a running foliage[1] which owes little or nothing to the acanthus, and the relative excellence in form and proportion of the animal and human figures, all of which are absent from the presumably contemporary carvings in the greater churches.

The origins, course, and chronology of this art are admittedly obscure and, in the nature of the case, must remain so, but its existence can hardly be denied when it is compared with those major works in which the Anglo-Norman carver might be expected to excel.

Finally, in the counties bordering on the still Celtic countries, there is evidence of a certain amount of Celtic influence which is commonly displayed in a lavish use of interlacement. This is to be seen particularly in Herefordshire and Shropshire; in the former county is a remarkable group of churches or remains of churches all of the same school, and several no doubt from the same hand. They may be approximately dated to about 1145 from the recorded facts of the building of one of them—Shobdon; most of them are directly connected with some Norman lordship and can thus be reasonably dissociated from any pre-Norman affinities. The queer form of figure-sculpture will be later touched upon, but the whole body of their ornament (Pl. 45) is so unusual and so isolated that it can only be explained by the operations of a single workshop[2] directed by a master of unusual originality.

[1] An early eleventh-century example of this foliage is to be found on Bishop Bernward's bronze doors at Hildesheim.

[2] The occurrence of this work at Leominster and its absence at Hereford seems to point to the former place as the head-quarters of the school, of which the best known example is the church of Kilpeck. Other works of the same

Enrichment of Orders and Mouldings

As has been already noted, with the exception of an occasional use of the billet and diaper ornament, the arch-orders and mouldings of the first period of Anglo-Norman work are entirely devoid of enrichment. The early years of the twelfth century, however, saw the introduction of the cheveron ornament, and this was closely followed by numerous other forms, which, used in combination, are responsible for the extreme richness of much twelfth-century work. Were it possible to date, at all closely, the introduction of the various forms, their chronological value would be obvious, but unfortunately it is only in certain cases that a definite conclusion can be arrived at.

The *Cheveron ornament* (or Zig-zag) is the most universal and characteristic of all Anglo-Norman forms of enrichment (Pls. 18, 24, and 29). It is formed either of reeding or fluting or of both combined and, in its later examples, often flanks or clasps the roll-moulding of an order. A further enrichment of the later work is obtained by carving the spandrels of the cheverons. In its simplest form it appears to have been introduced into England between the years 1110 and 1120. This is indicated by its absence from the eastern parts of Durham and its appearance in the nave, begun *c.* 1110; by its corresponding presence in the nave of Norwich, begun *c.* 1115, and its absence in the eastern parts of the church; by its presence in the choir of Hereford, begun *c.* 1110–15; and by its presence in the choir at Peterborough, begun in 1117, and the transept at Carlisle, *c.* 1123. It is significantly absent from those parts of other great churches such as Winchester and Ely, which can be definitely assigned to the eleventh or the very beginning of the twelfth century.

Cheveron ornament outlasted the twelfth century, but is used more sparingly in the later work, as may be seen in

type are the tympana at Stretton Sugwas, Brinsop, and Fownhope, arches at Rowlstone, and fonts at Castle Frome (Pl. 41) and Eardisley.

the final extension at Canterbury (1174–84) and in the church at Glastonbury (1184–*c.* 1200). Early thirteenth-century examples may be seen at Wells, north porch, and Hereford, Lady Chapel crypt.

The *Lozenge Ornament* is a variety, only, of the cheveron, formed by connecting two rows of cheverons. Good examples may be seen at Wymondham Abbey (nave) and Walsoken (chancel-arch).

The *Embattled Ornament* is also closely allied to the cheveron though it is always used in relief. It forms a bold break in the main lines of the arch, which is perhaps too emphatic to be pleasing. It appears in the reconstructed nave-clearstory of S. Étienne, Caen, *c.* 1130, and also in the nave of the Trinité, Caen, about the same date. In England there are good examples at Lincoln Cathedral, *c.* 1140–50 (west door), Kirkstall Abbey (west door), Bishop's Cleeve (Glos.), St. Margaret at Cliffe (Kent), Bockleton (Worcs.), and in Bishop Hugh de Puiset's work at Durham Cathedral and Castle.

The *Greek Key* (or Meander) *Ornament* is of the same general type as the cheveron and embattled ornaments. It is uncommon in this country but may be seen at St. David's Cathedral (nave), Hereford Cathedral (font), Compton Greenfields (Glos.), Barfreston (Kent), and elsewhere. A favourite form in France represented the pattern as in perspective, but this refinement hardly appears in England.

The *Disk Ornament* is most common in the eastern counties. The disks are either set flat, as at Haddiscoe (Norfolk) and Westhall (Suffolk), or, more commonly, on edge so that only half the circle is apparent. In the latter form it makes a very early appearance in Peterborough cloister, before the fire of 1118, and at a later date at Chedgrove, Heckingham, and Thurlton (Norfolk) and Braysworth (Suffolk).

The *Rosette Ornament* (Pl. 24) consists of a series of tangent or nearly tangent circles generally filled with concentric enrichment in the form of rosettes. An early example may be noted on the west doorway at Porchester Priory (Hants), founded in 1133. It also appears in the choir at Llandaff Cathedral, identified[1] with the church begun in 1120, but this seems an extremely early date for the elaborate ornament here displayed. Later examples may be cited in Hugh de Puiset's work at Durham Castle, the clearstory at Malmesbury Abbey, at Holt (Worcs.), and Hales (Norfolk). At Brayton (Yorks.), the circles, still set flat on the order, are filled with figure-carving, and form a step in the direction of the elaborate medallion enrichments of the mouldings at Malmesbury and Glastonbury, to be referred to later.

The *Chain Ornament* taking the form of a series of links like a chain, is uncommon, but occurs at St. John's, Chester (NE. arch), Stirchley (Salop), and in a modified form on the vault-ribs of the chancel of St. Peter's in the East, Oxford.

The *Twisted* or *Cable Ornament* (Pl. 24) is formed by a series of spiral grooves or reeds on a roll-moulding. Perhaps its earliest surviving example is in the transept at Southwell, *c.* 1120. On the west doorway of Castle Acre Priory it may be assigned to *c.* 1150, and there is a later example on the south doorway at Durham.

The *Beak-head* (Pls. 24 and 25), a curious and barbaric-looking ornament, takes the form of the head of a bird, beast, or monster, the beak or jaw of which appears to grip the moulding across which it is carved. There can be little doubt that the ultimate origin of the ornament is Scandinavian, but its particular application is probably English, as it is far more frequent and widely diffused in this country than elsewhere. It is seldom found in the cathedral or greater monastic churches, being largely confined to village churches, which would seem to imply that even in the twelfth century it was regarded as somewhat barbaric. Geographically[2] it is

[1] E. W. Lovegrove in *Brit. Arch. Ass. Journ.*, N.S., xxxv, p. 75.
[2] Leading examples may be noted at Brinkburn Priory (Northumberland),

PLATE 24

BRAYTON CHURCH, YORKS., DOORWAY
c. 1160

CASTLE ACRE PRIORY, W. FRONT
c. 1150

PLATE 25

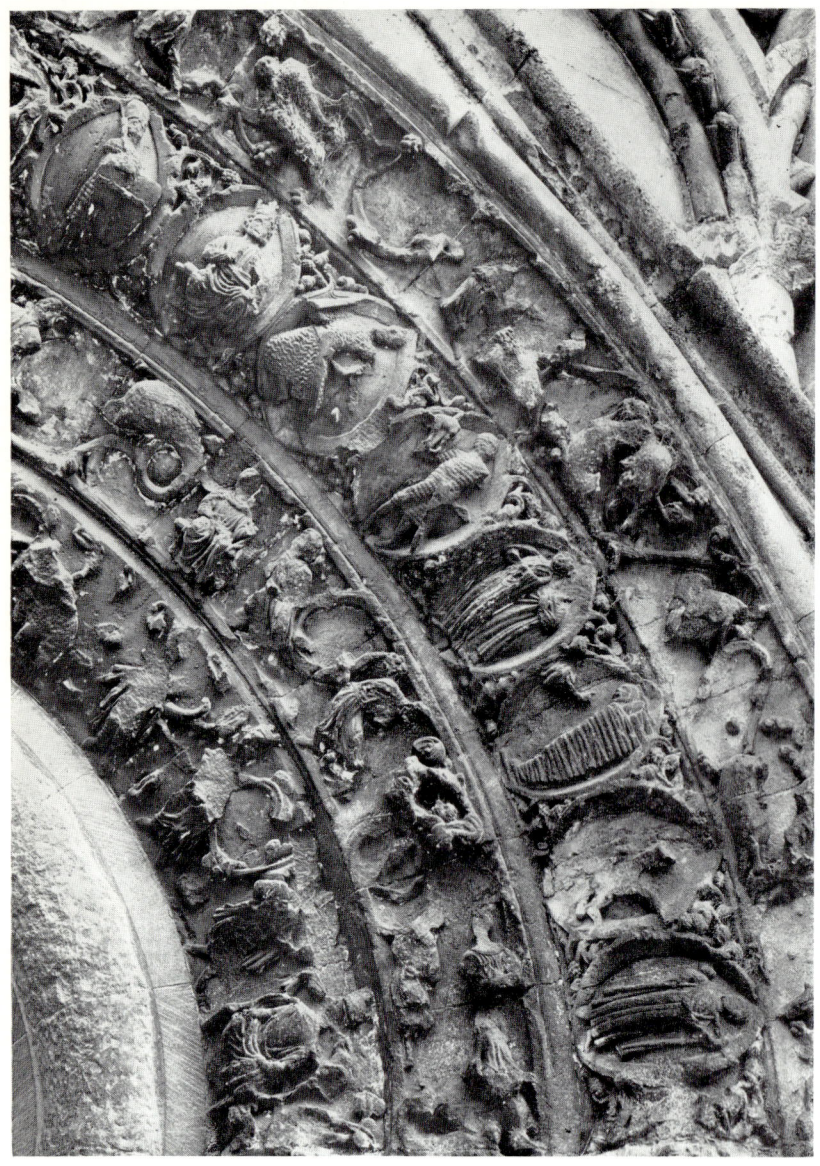

GLASTONBURY ABBEY, N. DOORWAY OF LADY CHAPEL
c. 1185–90

found pretty generally throughout the country except in the extreme south-east, where the counties of Essex, Kent, and Surrey appear to be almost devoid of examples. Its place is taken in Huntingdonshire by a local variety in which the animal form is absent, its place being taken by a wedge-shaped member scored with lines. Its date can only be arrived at by its architectural setting, for the example at Lincoln Cathedral is in the inserted west doorway of *c.* 1140–50, and the example from Kenilworth Abbey (now in the church) can only be said to be after the foundation in *c.* 1125. The general character of the buildings in which it occurs, indicates a central date of about 1150 for its employment, but an example on the north doorway at Southwell is perhaps earlier. The beak-head spread to Normandy, where it is not uncommon (e.g. Bayeux Cathedral, nave), and thence to the departments of the Oise and Aisne.[1]

In a reconstructed doorway at Easby Abbey (founded 1152) the beak-heads, in two rows, are rendered more naturalistically than usual and take the form of beast-heads.

The *Diaper Ornament* (Pl. 24 b), as applied to the orders of an arch, takes various forms, of which the following are the most usual: a plain chequer-pattern; a series of squares cut back in facets along the diagonals; and a series of panels or connected bands of interlacement. As an enrichment of the order of an arch all these would appear to belong to the first half of the twelfth century, though the second is otherwise employed as an ornament as early as the eleventh century.[2] The plain chequer may be seen at Broadwell

Adel, Stillingfleet, and Brayton (Yorks.), Steetley (Derby), Lincoln Cathedral, Holgate (Salop), Kilpeck (Hereford), Kenilworth (Warwick), Elkstone and S. Cerney (Glos.), Tickencote (Rutland), Barton St. Mary (Norfolk), Westhall (Suffolk), Bletchley (Bucks.), Iffley and Windrush (Oxon.), Lullington (Somerset), Bishop's Teignton (Devon), and Morwenstow (Cornwall).

[1] E. Lefèvre Pontalis in *Bull. Mon.*, lxx, p. 3.

[2] E.g. on the windows of the south transept at Winchester and perhaps still earlier at Notre-Dame-sur-l'eau Domfront.

(Glos.), the facetted squares at Castle Acre Priory, Hawksworth (Notts.) and Rowlstone (Hereford), and the interlacement at Northampton St. Peter, Hereford St. Giles's Hospital, and Dinton (Bucks.).

The *Billet, Reel, Pellet,* and other small enrichments are commonly confined to the smaller mouldings and need not be further particularized. A large version of the reel ornament is to be seen at Hales (Norfolk).

Transverse Mouldings. In occasional instances the inner order of an arch was enriched with a transverse moulding carried across each voussoir and giving a corrugated effect to the soffit, which is alike rich and unusual. The chancel-arch of the Templars' church at Garway (Hereford) is thus treated[1] and there is another example at Winchfield (Hants). At Steyning (Sussex) an arch of the nave (Pl. 18) has the mouldings of the cheveron ornament of the inner order, carried across the soffit, producing the same effect.

Carved Orders. The last half of the twelfth century produced the final phase in romanesque decoration of the orders of a doorway; this consisted of covering the entire order with carving generally disposed in a series of medallions. In the earlier examples, the subjects (generally Zodiacal symbols or the like) are strictly confined in a series of round panels or plaques, as may be seen at Brayton (Pl. 24), Alne, and Adel (Yorks.), and are set flat on the face of the order. At a later date (*c.* 1170–80) a different method was employed in two great churches of the west country— Malmesbury (south entrance) and Glastonbury (Pl. 25) (Lady chapel). Here the orders are rounded, and the whole surface is carved with a series of figure-subjects in low

---

[1] Precisely the same treatment is to be found at S. Wast Priory (Pas de Calais) and is ascribed by C. Enlart to a direct borrowing from the east where it occurs on the Bab el Foutouh at Cairo, *c.* 1090 (C. Enlart, *L'architecture romane dans la région picarde,* p. 214). An instance of the cusped arch, also derived from Islamic art and not uncommon in northern Spain and certain parts of France, is to be found in the south doorway of St. Anthony in Roseland, Cornwall (E. H. Sedding, *Norman Architecture in Cornwall,* Pl. IV), and also at Compton, Surrey.

relief enclosed in medallions of a much less pronounced character and forming a continuous design. The subjects are drawn from the Old Testament and the life of Christ; those on the south doorway at Glastonbury are unfinished, showing that they were carved when already in position.

Rich ornament of the same general character and of the same period is to be seen in a small group of Kentish churches. The south doorway at Barfreston, the best known of these, has two moulded orders covered with foliage-carving and a band of figures and foliage on the flat outer order. At Patrixbourne is a less elaborate example, and there is a third at St. Margaret at Cliffe. With these may be compared the foliage-carving on some of the orders of the west doorway at Rochester, and the equally elaborate carving with figures on the west doorway at Dunstable Priory (Beds.).

Intersecting Arcading. The decorative treatment of a wall-arcade, by springing the round arches from alternate piers, and thus forming a series of intersections, is one of the most characteristic and universal features of Anglo-Norman work. It is not, however, present in the earliest work, but is to be found at Durham (choir-aisles begun 1093) (Pl. 26), Norwich (south transept, east side), *c.* 1110, and at about the same date at Christchurch (north transept). The perhaps unique example of the intersection of three arches in the same manner at St. John's, Devizes, has already been noted. Late in the twelfth century a refinement was occasionally introduced, by intersecting not only the arches but the mouldings of the arches as well; this may be seen in the presbytery at Bolton Priory[1] (Yorks.), at Bishop's Cleeve (Glos.), porch,[2] and elsewhere.

Cylindrical Piers. The ornamentation of the surface of large cylindrical piers by grooved lines forming spiral flutings, lozenges, or zig-zags is first found in the choir at

---

[1] *Bolton Priory,* Thoresby Soc., xxx, p. 137.
[2] *Brist. and Glos. Arch. Soc. Trans.,* l, p. 95.

Durham before the end of the eleventh century. The work here and in the nave at Durham (Frontispiece) was copied in churches directly affected by the Durham influence such as Lindisfarne Priory, a cell of Durham (*c.* 1120–5), and Dunfermline Abbey[1] (*c.* 1125–30). It also appears in the naves of Norwich Cathedral, Selby Abbey, and Waltham Collegiate church (later Abbey), and in the parish church of Kirkby Lonsdale (Westmorland). In the middle of the twelfth century or later the same ornament was revived with the difference that the lines were embossed on the surface instead of sunk below it. This variety is to be found at Orford[2] (Suffolk), Pittington (Durham), and Compton Martin (Somerset).

Capitals and Bases. The normal type of Anglo-Norman capital is the cubical, in the form commonly called the cushion-capital. In this form it is almost unknown in Normandy before the Conquest. Its general adoption in England is thus the more surprising, for though it was used by the later Anglo-Saxons and probably borrowed from Germany, its use was not so general as to be likely to influence the succeeding style.

The simplest form of this capital, with a single curve on each face, was soon elaborated. The double,[3] or even triple, curve, each carried down to the necking in a semi-cone, forming the earliest form of scalloped capital, appeared before the close of the eleventh century, and its elaboration continued throughout the twelfth century. The evolution of this scalloped, fluted, or gadrooned capital has been treated by Dr. John Bilson,[4] but its more elaborate forms are confined to the middle and second half of the twelfth century. A twelfth-century feature is the introduction of

---

[1] Macgibbon and Ross, *Ecclesiastical Architecture of Scotland*, i, p. 230.
[2] The feature, at this place, is really a series of small attached shafts carried spirally round the main pier.   [3] E.g. St. John's chapel, Tower of London.
[4] 'Le chapiteau à godron en Angleterre'. *Cong. Arch. de France*, Caen, 1908, ii, p. 634. See also E. Sharpe, *The Ornamentation of the Transitional Period of Brit. Architecture* (1871).

PLATE 26

DURHAM CATHEDRAL, WALL-ARCADING
late 11th century

ROCHESTER CATHEDRAL, NORMAN CRYPT
early 12th century

PLATE 27

SONNING, BERKS., CAPITALS FROM
READING ABBEY

mid 12th century

reeding in the angles between the scallop-stems or cones, and a final development rendered the whole motif as a piece of crinkled ribbon, as in the capitals from Bridlington cloister, now in the church. In the west country the scalloped capitals of the late period assume a concave curve to the stems.

The simple cushion-capital was frequently retained in work later than the eleventh century as a field for carving a form for which it was eminently suited. We have already referred to the possibly early examples of such carving at Westminster Hall, Hereford, and (accompanied by the volute) Southwell, but the best collection of such carvings is to be found in the crypt at Canterbury. The structure dates from the close of the eleventh century, but the carving is generally attributed to about 1140, many of the capitals being either unfinished or untouched. The subjects are mainly of a monstrous or mythological nature, and are of a refinement and quality of carving which partake far more of the nature of contemporary foreign work than any other English carving. The 'historied' capital carved with figure-subjects of scriptural or moral nature, so common in French romanesque, is little seen in England. With few exceptions[1] the figure-subjects here are of little or no significance and indicate only the fancy of the carver.[2]

The true Norman volute-capital (Pls. 2 and 15), as has been said, is a fairly common feature in this country. It appears in some of our earliest Anglo-Norman buildings and survived in occasional instances well into the twelfth century.[3] At the Tower of London it is accompanied by an unusual flat decoration on the faces of the capital, in the form of a T-cross.[4] At Canterbury are some crude capitals with

[1] E.g. The Judgement of Solomon (Westminster Cloister), the Harrowing of Hell (Hereford presbytery).
[2] E.g. Castor and Wakerley (Northants), Bretforton (Worcs.), &c.
[3] E.g. St. John's chapel in the Tower, Durham Castle chapel, Gloucester crypt, Blyth Priory, Lastingham crypt, and Amberley (Sussex) chancel-arch.
[4] This also occurs on the early monastic buildings at Westminster and in the crypt at Canterbury Cathedral.

rows of subsidiary leaves probably from the church of Lanfranc. Similar capitals may be seen in the presbytery-triforium at Norwich in conjunction with other motifs, which together form perhaps the most varied collection of early Norman capitals to be seen in this country.

Bases.[1] The only ornamental feature of the moulded base is the angular binding-projection, commonly called a claw or spur ornament, passing over the moulding and on to the angle of the square plinth. It makes its appearance quite early in the twelfth century, as a simple leaf or band, on the east presbytery-arch at Hereford, and on the crossing-piers at Bath. Later in the century it adopted a scrolled water-leaf form often of considerable elegance and simplicity, but achieved its most remarkable development in the elaborate palmette-bosses in the crypt of Archbishop Roger's church at York.

Tympana. A collection of all the most important Anglo-Norman tympana has been brought together and published by the late Mr. Charles Keyser.[2] A few may be added to the series but little of importance seems to have escaped his attention. The custom of filling in with solid masonry the round arch of a door-head was perhaps coming into fashion before the Conquest, and there are a number of examples still surviving which may well date from before that event. Those at Hoveringham (Notts.) and Knook (Wilts.) have decoration which seems definitely of pre-Conquest character, while those at St. Nicholas, Ipswich, have Saxon inscriptions, and a third at Pennington (Lincs.) has an inscription in runes.

The earliest post-Conquest tympana are generally of the simplest character, sometimes consisting of a plain un-

---

[1] Two instances have been noted in England of the Italian practice of setting the base of a shaft on the back of a crouching lion or other animal. One of these perhaps came from St. John's Abbey, Colchester (*Antiq. Journ.*, vi, p. 450), the other is in the church of Sutton by Castor (Northants). The motif belongs rightly to the twelfth century or earlier, but both the English examples date from the early part of the thirteenth century.

[2] C. Keyser, *Norman Tympana and Lintels*, 2nd edit., 1927.

PLATE 28

TUTBURY PRIORY, W. DOORWAY
c. 1180

ROCHESTER CATHEDRAL, W. DOORWAY
c. 1160–70

PLATE 29

BARFRESTON CHURCH, KENT,
S. DOORWAY
c. 1170–80

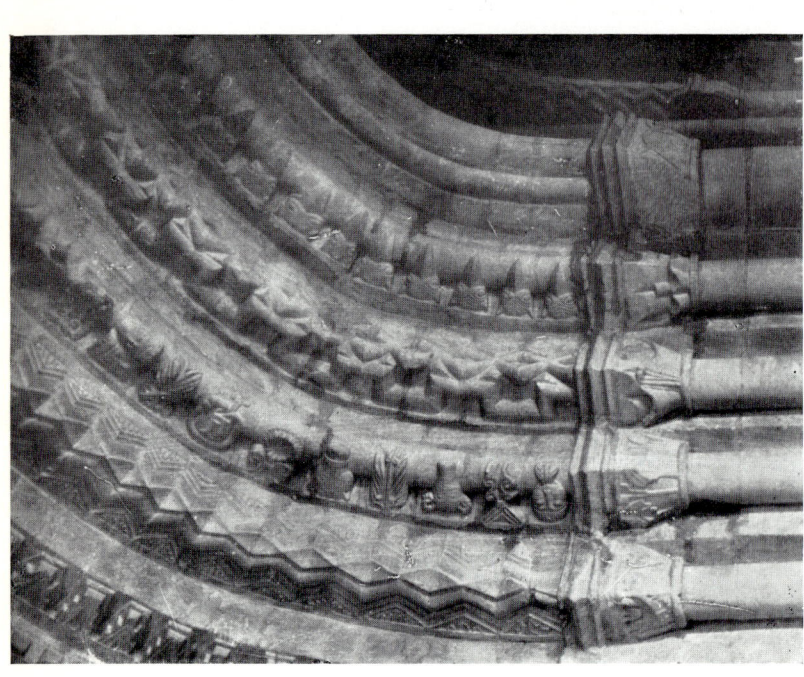

TICKENCOTE CHURCH, RUTLAND,
CHANCEL ARCH
c. 1160–70

sculptured stone, as at Tedstone Wafer (Hereford), and sometimes of built squares of masonry set diagonally above the lintel, as at Winstone (Glos.) and Bury (Hunts.). A number of very crude carvings may also date from an early period, but these on the other hand may only be examples of rustic work of a later date. The fact that in such churches as Durham, Ely, and Lincoln, enriched mid-twelfth-century and later doorways were inserted in the earlier work would seem to imply that the work they replaced was as devoid of ornament as the corresponding features in the early churches of Normandy. As a rule the sculptured tympana in English churches belong then to the twelfth century, and the great majority of them to the last three-quarters of that century.

Considering the field of choice open to the sculptor they display an extraordinary lack of variety in subject. Thus the life of Christ is represented by a single example of the Adoration of the Magi at Bishop's Teignton (Pl. 32) (Devon), and a single example of the Entry into Jerusalem at Aston Eyre (Salop). Symbolical representations of Christ on the other hand are numerous. The conventional 'Majesty' in a vesica with attendant angels or the evangelists has important examples at Rochester (Pl. 28) (west doorway), and Elkstone (Glos.) with evangelists, and at Ely (cloister), Malmesbury, Water Stratford (Bucks.), Rowlstone (Hereford), and Pedmore (Worcs.) with angels. The central figure in the tympanum (Pl. 29) at Barfreston (Kent) is surrounded by scroll-work with angels, the heads of a king and queen, and other figures. There are numerous examples of the Agnus Dei, at Gloucester St. Nicholas, Thwing (Yorks.), Preston (Glos.), and elsewhere, and a number of instances of the Good Shepherd theme (e.g. Hognaston (Derby), Stony Stanton (Leics.), and Little Paxton (Hunts.)). The Harrowing of Hell appears at Shobdon (Hereford), Beckford (Glos.), and Quenington (Glos.). A very stylized figure of the Virgin and Child at Fownhope (Hereford) is remarkable as showing the Virgin giving the blessing and provided with a cruciform nimbus as well as the Child. At Siddington (Glos.) is a figure of Christ giving the Keys to St. Peter and the Book to St. Paul.

Old Testament subjects are very infrequent, but there are spirited representations of Samson and the lion (Pl. 34) at Stretton Sugwas (Hereford) and Highworth (Wilts.), and Daniel in the lions' den at Shalfleet (I. of W.) and Downe St. Mary (Devon).

Figures of individual saints appear to be confined to St. Michael, St. George, and St. Peter. The first, combatting the dragon, is not uncommon and may be seen at Moreton Valence (Glos.), Hallaton (Leics.), and Kingswinford (Staffs.). The companion subject of St. George on horseback is represented at Brinsop (Hereford) and Ruardean (Glos.); the same saint in the less familiar setting of the fight at Antioch (Pl. 30) is shown on a tympanum at Damerham (Wilts.) and Fordington (Dorset). St. Peter with his key appears only once, at Handborough (Oxon.).

A few tympana bear figures of monsters such as the mermaid at Stow ʼLonga (Hunts.), and the Sagittarius at Stokesub-Hamdon (Somerset), and Kencott (Oxon.).

A considerable number of other examples bear figures of greater or less crudity to which it would be idle to assign more significance than the whim of the carver or the half understood instructions which he received.

In addition to those carved with figures a large number of tympana are enriched with simple crosses of various forms, sprays of foliage more or less conventionalized, or diaper work of various types such as scale ornament and chequerpattern. Amongst the most curious of these is one at Shirburn (Oxon.) which is covered with a design of threestrand interlacement. A re-used tympanum at Castor (Northants) is filled with a dedication inscription of 1124, which, apart from its value as dating a remarkable church, is an interesting example of lettering.

PLATE 30

FORDINGTON CHURCH, DORSET, CARVING OVER S. DOORWAY
mid 12th century

PLATE 31

NORWICH CATHEDRAL, FIGURE OVER
N. TRANSEPT DOORWAY

c. 1110

Diaper ornament is also occasionally employed in the tympana of triforium arcades; an example with scale ornament can be seen at Christchurch (Hants), and others with chequer-pattern in the naves of Rochester, Selby, and Chichester; at the last place there is also a more elaborate diapering of four-leaved flowers. A diaper of minute arches covers the face of the gable over the doorway of the gate-tower at Bury St. Edmunds (Pl. 10), and one of conjoined circles in the gables of Bishop Alexander's rudimentary west transept at Lincoln.

Diapering of the actual wall surfaces, apart from the small enclosed spaces referred to above, is very uncommon. A good instance occurs, however, on the central tower (Pl. 21) of Castor (Northants), where both the scale and the diagonal chequer are employed and which, as we have seen, can be dated to 1124. The circular stair-turret of the north transept at Christchurch provides a minor example.

Sculpture.[1] The history of the development of Anglo-Norman figure-sculpture is one of the most difficult to disentangle in the whole history of art, not only because of the almost entire absence of dated examples, but also because of the conflicting and concurrent influences which were brought to bear upon it. Of these we have at least three which may be considered of first-class importance in the study of the subject: (*a*) the Anglo-Saxon tradition; (*b*) the unaided Norman attempt; and (*c*) the more or less matured styles which filtered in from southern France.

The first of these, the Saxon tradition, was unequal, geographically, in its strength, for two reasons. The Danish invasions had either blotted out or greatly weakened the Saxon tradition in those eastern and northern counties which were most subject to their inroads or had longest remained under their direct control, and the Danes in common with the other Scandinavian races had no figure-sculpture of their own. Operating in a similar way but over

[1] Prior and Gardner, *Medieval Figure Sculpture in England.*

a different and wider geographical area, the Norman Conquest had a similar result. The Normanization of England (if we may so put it) was more complete in the south-eastern half of the country than in the other parts, where the Normans were, for long, more politically than culturally supreme the farther they went from the Channel ports. The stronghold of Anglo-Saxon art immediately before the Conquest was undoubtedly the old kingdom of Wessex with its capital at Winchester, and though its influence was felt throughout the kingdom during the peaceful reign of Edward the Confessor, Wessex was actually the only part in which this art had firm root. After the Conquest, we should thus expect to find more trace of this tradition in those parts of Wessex most remote from direct Norman influence and in those parts of the west which were least touched by the earlier Danish inroads.

The Normans themselves brought with them, as we have seen, only the crudest ideas of figure-sculpture or indeed of architectural ornament of any description, and consequently those parts of England which were most thoroughly Normanized remained longest without sculpture of any but the Norman standard. The Anglo-Normans, however, gradually evolved a figure-sculpture of their own, which, though often decoratively effective, was largely lacking in any but the crudest ideas of drawing or proportion.

The third influence took its rise from the renaissance of figure-sculpture in the south of France towards the end of the eleventh century, and did not make its influence felt in England until a considerably later date. The introduction of the Cluniac order into England late in the eleventh century may have later provided a channel for the passage of Burgundian and South French art and sculpture into England, but the main stream extended itself gradually through northern France and hardly reached England before the middle of the twelfth century.

It is obvious that none of these three influences operated on clear-cut lines, and the apparently haphazard survival of many of the examples is not often to be accounted for.

The Saxon tradition would appear to show itself in at least two forms, the first purely sculptural and closely akin to the larger sculptures of the pre-Conquest period,[1] the second a flat-surface treatment in very low relief which is distinguished by a fair standard in drawing and proportion. This is directly descended from earlier carvings (such as those at Southwell and Hoveringham), involving dragon-esque forms and foliage which are a combination of Anglo-Saxon and Scandinavian motives. The great majority of examples of both these types are to be found in the counties of the middle west.

The sculptural type, slightly heavy in its masses, is generally well-balanced in its composition and correct in its drawing. It is exemplified in the tympana at Tredington (Pl. 32) and Little Barrington (Glos.), Aston Eyre (Salop), and in the Harrowing of Hell at Shobdon[2] (Hereford), and on the lead fonts of Dorchester (Oxon.) (Pl. 41) and Walton (Surrey).

The low-relief type is more widely spread; it often exhibits a capacity for portraying motion which is entirely absent from works of the Norman school. The tympana at Moreton Valence (Glos.), Hallaton (Leics.), Fordington (Dorset) (Pl. 31), and Highworth (Wilts.) (Pl. 34 b) are good examples, and the last may be compared with the purely Norman rendering (Pl. 34 a) of the same subject (Samson and the lion) at Stretton Sugwas (Hereford). To the same class belong the Labours of the Months on the fonts at Burnham Deepdale (Norfolk) in stone, and at Brookland (Kent) in lead.

---

[1] In this connexion attention may be called to the recently discovered Majesty at Barnack, which is an advanced example of this type, probably of late pre-Conquest date and exemplifying the stucco-tradition. *Antiq. Journ.* xiii, p. 468.
[2] Curiously enough the two other tympana at the same place are of a different type.

Pure Norman figure-sculpture begins in England with such attempts as that already noted in the castle-chapel at Durham (1072). With this may be compared the almost equally crude figures on the tympana at Little Paxton (Hunts.) and Beckford (Glos.), or on the fonts at Curdworth (Warwick), Fincham (Norfolk), or Cowlam (Yorks.). The standard of execution gradually improved, but at least to the middle of the twelfth century the Norman carver appears to have been quite incapable of grasping the simplest principles of proportion or anatomy. As a result we have the stunted oddities on the tympanum (Pl. 32) at Bishop's Teignton (Devon) and the dislocated Samson on that at Stretton Sugwas (Hereford) in direct connexion with the richest examples of architectural ornament. The curious Hereford-shire school, already referred to, to which this Stretton Sugwas tympanum (Pl. 34) belongs is one of the few cases in which a distinctively local style can be definitely recognized. In spite of the inherent weaknesses of all Norman sculpture, the local master has here achieved some measure of success partly by making most of his figures an integral part of his decorative scheme, as in the tympanum at Fownhope, the font at Castle Frome, and the south doorway at Kilpeck, and partly by an individualistic treatment of the figures themselves, which intrigues the eye by its unfamiliar conventions. In these, however, as in all other examples of the type, the figure remains at worst an ill-formed doll, and at best an attractive marionette.

The influence of the renaissance of south French sculpture is perhaps first definitely seen in the carved capitals of the crypt at Canterbury which, as we have seen, are generally assigned to about 1140. The human figures they contain, such as Samson and the lion, are entirely sophisticated examples of the French art of the period, such as appear only occasionally elsewhere in England. To the same influence, perhaps transmitted through Cluniac channels, belongs the remarkable series of carved capitals (Pl. 27)

PLATE 32

TREDINGTON CHURCH, GLOS., TYMPANUM
early 12th century

BISHOP'S TEIGNTON CHURCH, DEVON, TYMPANUM
mid 12th century

PLATE 33

ELY CATHEDRAL, W. DOORWAY FROM CLOISTER
c. 1170. *Photograph Starr and Rignall, Ely*

MALMESBURY ABBEY, FIGURES OF APOSTLES IN
S. PORCH
c. 1170–80

from Reading.[1] The south French sculptors achieved some
of their greatest triumphs in the great tympana depicting in
some form or another the apocalyptic vision of the Last
Judgement. Many of these date from the first quarter of
the twelfth century, but, as M. Mâle[2] has shown, the idea
did not penetrate into northern France before the erection
of the west portals of S. Denis by Abbot Suger between 1133
and 1140, and thence to Chartres. The simple and not uncommon form of the English tympanum, carved with a
Majesty accompanied by angels or the apocalyptic beasts
(the only form in which the theme appears in England)
appears certainly in the first half of the twelfth century, but
the finest English example, that over the west door (Pl. 28)
at Rochester (where it is accompanied by the traditional
figures of Solomon and the Queen of Sheba carved on the
jambs), is so definitely North French in inspiration that it
must be dated at about 1160–70. A Majesty of the same
period and ultimate origin, but probably carved in the
Norman tradition, is to be seen over the prior's door at Ely
(Pl. 33). Its anatomical absurdities are obvious, but they
seem to be almost intentional and adopted with a view to
decorative effect, like the abnormalities of heraldic beasts.

The gradual improvement of the Norman carver and
the infiltration of French art, combined to produce in the
latter half of the twelfth century a much higher level of
figure-sculpture than had before been possible. This is
exemplified in the figures of the Virtues on the fonts at
Stanton Fitzwarren (Wilts.) and Southrop (Glos.) (Pl. 42),
and in the Last Supper on the font at Brighton. Elaborate
scrolls with figures and beasts, excellently rendered in the
French manner, appear also on the jamb-shafts of the west
door at Lincoln, and on the font at Porchester (Hants), and
with these come the minute and elaborate figure-subjects
in medallions which enrich the doorways of the porch at

---

[1] *Proc. Soc. Ants.*, xxviii, p. 234.
[2] E. Mâle, *L'Art religieux du XIIe siècle en France*, p. 178.

Malmesbury (*c.* 1170–80) and the Lady Chapel at Glastonbury (*c.* 1186). In immediate connexion with this work at
Malmesbury, we find a series of apostles (Pl. 33) whose stiff-
necked figures display, even at this late period, some of the
graceless features of Norman sculpture.

A further important example of the period is the series of
carved panels with scenes from the Old Testament and the
Last Judgement, on the west front at Lincoln. The panels
seem to have been disarranged, but whatever their original
position, they appear to belong to the middle or second
half of the twelfth century and perhaps formed the completion of Bishop Alexander's (died 1148) work on the nave
and west front. They are by more than one hand, and are
remarkable as the only Anglo-Norman example of anything in the nature of a frieze-sculpture which has survived
in this country.

The surviving monumental effigies of the twelfth century
fall into place in the above classification. Nearly all of them
belong to the latter part of the century, and thus display
the work of a sophisticated age. This may be seen in the
figures at Peterborough, Sherborne, and elsewhere, but
occasionally the awkward hand of the Norman carver is
apparent, as in the crude bishop's figure at Exeter, and in
an even cruder figure of an abbot of Neubo[1] dating from as
late as about 1200.

---

[1] *Antiq. Journ.,* xi, p. 65.

PLATE 34

STRETTON SUGWAS CHURCH, HEREFORDSHIRE, TYMPANUM
c. 1150

HIGHWORTH CHURCH, WILTS., TYMPANUM
c. 1160

Chapter X

CHURCH DECORATION AND FITTINGS IN THE TWELFTH CENTURY

THE review of church decoration and fittings will be confined to those actually forming part of the structure, or such as are in the nature of the case fixtures in the building. Portable objects, besides being few in number, are often of uncertain provenance and can have no place in an architectural treatise. With the exception of fonts the surviving twelfth-century fittings are comparatively few in number, but the exception makes up for the scarcity in the other classes by a profusion of examples which is perhaps unparalleled in any other country. The examples of wall-painting include a few of outstanding merit, and the monuments provide an interesting if somewhat attenuated series.

Painted Decoration.[1] The damp climate of England has been more fatal to the great majority of medieval wall-painting in this country than any actively hostile action of protestant, puritan, or church-warden. These latter were responsible only for concealment, by successive coats of whitewash, of the pictures which were already deteriorating from the inevitable leaky roof or crumbling mortar. English wall-painting was invariably applied to the plaster of the walls after it had dried, and not, in the manner of true fresco, while it was still wet; this again was a circumstance unfavourable to permanency, and it is rather surprising that so much has survived than that so much has disappeared.

It is reasonably certain that every twelfth-century ecclesiastical building received or was intended to receive painted

---

[1] C. E. Keyser, *A List of Buildings in Great Britain and Ireland having Painted Decorations*, 3rd edit., 1883; T. Borenius and E. W. Tristram, *English Medieval Painting*, 1927.

U

decoration of one sort or another. In the simplest buildings this, no doubt, was often confined to lining up the plastered surfaces to imitate masonry, both plaster and masonry lines being commonly continued over ashlar and rubble alike. Occasionally arches were painted with alternate voussoirs of differing colour, as in the central-tower of St. Albans, and in many cases the mouldings were picked out in various tints and the plain surfaces enriched with cheveron bands, or one of the many forms of diapered ornament.[1] The details of these enrichments are instructive, as the painter evidently copied from manuscripts rather than buildings. Thus in wall-paintings we encounter the crinkled ribbon pattern at Canterbury Cathedral, a form of pelta pattern at Chaldon (Surrey), and a rich acanthus frieze at Durham Galilee, which hardly make their appearance in English twelfth-century building. The canopies painted over figures, again, are copied direct from manuscript originals, and show the turreted groups of buildings, which also appear on some of the tomb-slabs. Another favourite form of decoration was the painted representation of hanging cloths or curtains; these formed a high dado at Durham Galilee and Barfreston chancel, while at Hardham (Sussex) some of the figure-subjects are represented as painted on hanging cloths.

In a few instances it is possible to form some idea of the complete scheme of painted decoration of a twelfth-century church, and of these the most notable are Copford (Essex), Kempley (Glos.), Hardham (Sussex), Barfreston (Kent), and Durham Galilee. At Copford,[2] the paintings of the apse and chancel-arch, though much restored, are complete; the apse has a Majesty surrounded by angels on the vault, a series of apostles under arcades below, and geometrical ornament in bands round the windows; the

[1] Architectural decoration of this nature exists or existed at Durham Galilee, Norwich presbytery, Rochester (nave), Canterbury (crypt), Bishop's Wilton, Kempley, Elstow (destroyed), Chester Cathedral, and numerous other places.
[2] *Roy. Com. on Hist. Mons., Essex*, iii, p. 77.

PLATE 35

DURHAM, GALILEE, PAINTED FRIEZE
c. 1180

DURHAM, GALILEE, PAINTING
OF BISHOP
c. 1180

PLATE 36

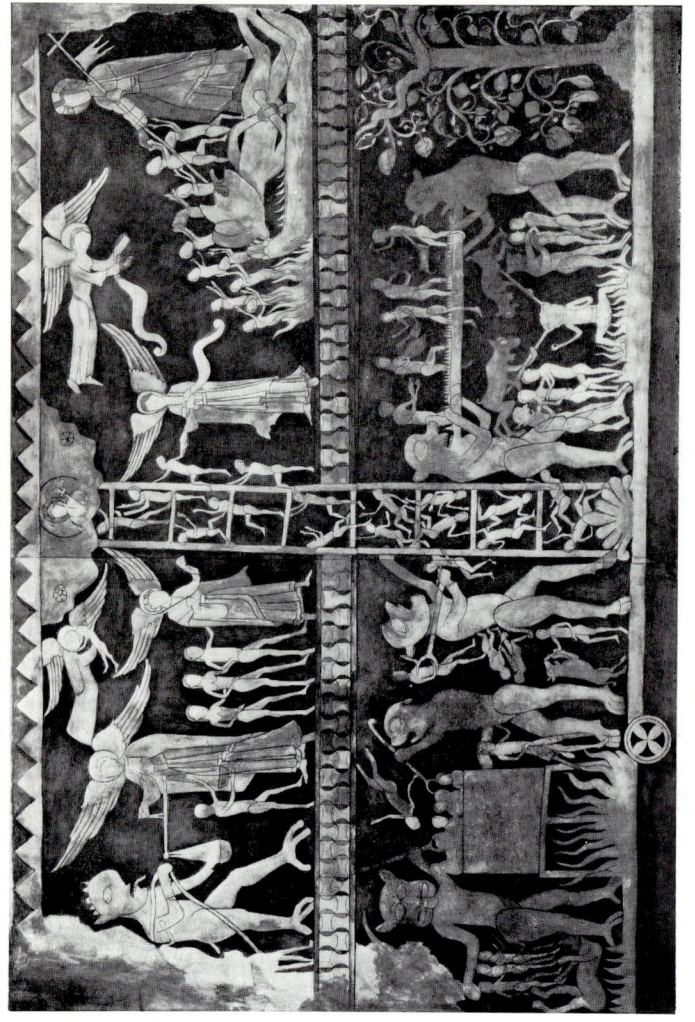

CHALDON CHURCH, SURREY, PAINTING OF THE DOOM

late 12th century

PLATE 37

BARFRESTON, KENT, PAINTINGS FORMERLY IN CHANCEL

c. 1180

PLATE 38

CANTERBURY CATHEDRAL, PAINTING IN ST. ANSELM'S
CHAPEL, ST. PAUL AND THE VIPER

c. 1150–60

soffit of the chancel-arch bears the signs of the Zodiac. Elsewhere in the church the subjects are fragmentary. The chancel at Kempley[1] has a barrel-vault, and this and the side walls are painted with a Majesty with the evangelists and apostles (Pl. 46) under arcades on each side below the main subject; on the east wall is a bishop. At Hardham[2] both chancel and nave have extensive remains of their twelfth-century decoration. These consist mainly of figure-subjects and include the Fall, the Elders of the Apocalypse, scenes from the Life and Passion of Christ, St. George at Antioch, and the Torments of Hell. The inscriptions and the costume in the battle-scene of St. George at Antioch indicate that these paintings belong to the first half of the twelfth century. The Barfreston paintings[3] (Pl. 37) were confined to the chancel and were destroyed when the church was rebuilt. They consisted of a curtained dado with a range of heads in medallions as a frieze, the Adoration of the Magi and various figures of bishops and ladies in the window-splays, and a range of figures of angels and bishops, forming a frieze over the windows in the east wall. These paintings must date from the last quarter of the twelfth century.

The Galilee at Durham[4] retains considerable but very fragmentary remains of its decorations (Pl. 35). These include a high painted curtain on the east wall with a remarkably rich frieze of acanthus leaves, figures of a king and a bishop, and a figure-subject. These must date from just after the building of the Galilee, c. 1175.

Of individual subjects which survive, the most important, from every point of view, is the panel representing St. Paul and the viper (Pl. 38) in St. Anselm's chapel in Canterbury Cathedral.[5] It is of mid-twelfth-century date, and both in

[1] J. T. Micklethwaite in *Arch.*, xlvi, p. 187.
[2] P. M. Johnston in *Sussex Arch. Colls.*, xliv, p. 73.
[3] Library of Soc. of Ants. London, Red Portfolio, Kent, i.
[4] *Ibid.*, Durham.
[5] Often illustrated, e.g. Tristram and Borenius, *op. cit.*, Pl. 3; *Arch.*, lii, p. 389, &c.

design and execution is equal to anything of its age in Europe. In St. Gabriel's chapel in the crypt at Canterbury is a series of paintings of rather later date.[1] They represent the birth and naming of St. John the Baptist, a Majesty, angels, &c. In the Infirmary chapel, at the same place, are remains of a fine Virgin and Child and saints with enriched borders.[2] The remaining examples to be noted are of greater iconographical than artistic interest, they form part of the decoration of remote country churches where a high level of attainment is not to be expected. At Chaldon[3] (Surrey) is a Last Judgement and Purgatorial Ladder (Pl. 36), and at Patcham[4] (Sussex) is a more conventional rendering of a Last Judgement or Doom. At Westmeston[5] in the same county are a Flagellation, Descent from the Cross, St. Paul and St. Peter receiving the book and keys from Christ, and other subjects, and at Pyrford[6] (Surrey) are some unusual subjects from the story of Jezebel, and earlier scenes from the Old Testament. At Claverley[7] (Salop) the whole of the north wall of the nave is occupied by a large subject, identified by Dr. Borenius as a Psychomachia or Combat of the Virtues and Vices. There are fourteen horses and riders in combat, with kite-shaped shields.

The surviving painted woodwork of the twelfth century is practically confined to the canted ceiling of the nave at Peterborough.[8] This ceiling (Pl. 46) is divided into a series of lozenge-shaped panels by painted mouldings, and the panels themselves contain seated figures of kings and bishops, apostles, &c., in the middle row and at the sides, players on instruments and grotesques. The whole of the work has been much repainted.

[1] Tristram and Borenius, *op. cit.*, Pl. 4.   [2] *Arch.*, lxiii, p. 51.

[3] J. G. Waller in *Surrey Arch. Cols.*, v, p. 275, and G. C. Druce, *ibid.*, xxiii, p. 1.

[4] C. E. Keyser in *Arch. Journ.*, xxxviii, p. 80.

[5] C. H. Campion in *Sussex Arch. Cols.*, xvi, p. 1.

[6] *V.C.H., Surrey*, iii, p. 435 (no illustration).

[7] *Arch. Journ.*, lx, p. 51, and Tristram and Borenius, *op. cit.*, p. 4 (read Claver ley for Chalgrove).

[8] W. Strickland, *The Ancient Painted Ceiling of the Nave of Peterborough.*

Screens. In the greater churches of the twelfth century, the choir was commonly bounded on the west by a solid stone screen or pulpitum. In addition to this, in monastic churches, there was a second screen called the Rood-screen farther west, sometimes of wood, and sometimes of masonry also. The pulpitum had a central doorway while the rood-screen had two doorways with the nave-altar between them. Foundations of several of these structures have been uncovered, and the twelfth-century pulpitum, at Ely, remained standing until the close of the eighteenth century. Sketches of it were made before its destruction, and from these the late Sir Wm. Hope made a reconstruction.[1] It had a central and two side doorways, connected by arcading, and a parapet with quatrefoiled panels divided by pilasters.

Carved fragments, conjectured to have formed part of the Rood-screen at Durham, have come to light in the neighbourhood of the cathedral. The Rites of Durham[2] describes this screen as having the whole story and Passion of our Lord wrought in stone and gilt and the story and pictures of the twelve apostles above. The surviving panels represent scenes in the garden after the Resurrection.

Of screens in the minor churches, which, if they existed at all, were commonly of wood, there are no surviving remains, though a wooden balustrade of round arches with late twelfth-century shafts and capitals stands on the front of the vault of the remarkable lower chancel at Compton (Surrey)[3] already referred to.

Stained Glass. The use of coloured glass in the windows of churches was perhaps introduced as far back as the sixth century,[4] and an example of the ninth century has actually been found in the Carolingian cemetery of Séry-lès-Mézières

---

[1] *Arch.*, lxvii, Pl. IX.

[2] *Rites of Durham* (Surtees Soc., vol. 107), p. 33.

[3] Parker, *Gloss. of Arch.* (Plates), Pl. 181.

[4] See O. M. Dalton's edition of Gregory of Tours, *The History of the Franks*, i, p. 328. Gregory himself, however, makes no reference to colour, but mentions glass windows in wooden frames at Yseure (*Lib. in gloria martyrum beatorum*, 58).

(Aisne).[1] It has a simple cross with pendent Alpha and Omega after the manner of the age, and set in lead. It seems doubtful if any glass, now existing, showing figures can be dated earlier than the twelfth century, and in England the earliest surviving glass does not go back beyond about 1170–80. The glass of this period forms a mosaic of various coloured pieces on which the lines were applied in a brown or yellow composition, burnt in. The joints are formed by strips of double-grooved lead, called cames, and the whole mosaic is attached to an iron frame following the outline of the window, and frequently subdivided by circles and lozenges which frame the chief subjects or panels of the glass.

The two chief collections of twelfth-century English glass are those which formed part of the original glazing of Archbishop Roger's choir at York, finished c. 1170, and the rebuilt and extended choir of Canterbury, finished in 1184. The York collection[2] is very fragmentary and is now preserved in various windows of the nave clearstory. It includes a considerable amount of borders of elaborate acanthus ornament, a large seated figure under a canopy, and one panel of a Jesse tree with a figure of a king, which may be compared with the rather earlier examples of the same subject at S. Denis and Chartres.

The collection at Canterbury Cathedral[3] consists of some thirty-four figures (out of sixty-four), formerly filling the clearstory of the choir and representing the genealogy of Christ. Each figure (Pl. 39) has the name of the person represented, at the back. They are now distributed in various windows in the church and their place in the clearstory taken by modern copies.

---

[1] *Bull. Mon.* (1910), pp. 5–23.

[2] J. Browne, *Hist. of St. Peter's, York*, ii, Pls. CXIX, CXXIII, and CXXVIII. W. R. Lethaby in *Arch. Journ.*, lxxii, p. 37. N. H. J. Westlake, *The History of Design in Painted Glass*, 1881, i, chap. ix.

[3] *Notes on the Painted Glass in Canterbury Cathedral* (E. Williams), 1897, and A. J. Mason, *A Guide to the Ancient Glass in Canterbury Cathedral*, 1925.

PLATE 39

CANTERBURY CATHEDRAL, GLASS FIGURE
OF METHUSELAH FROM THE CHOIR
CLEARSTORY
c. 1185–90

Other possible examples of twelfth-century glass are to be found at Lincoln Cathedral and Dorchester Abbey.[1]

Doors and their Fittings. The only door, so far noticed in England, which can be reasonably assigned to the age before the Conquest is that in the north doorway of Hadstock church, Essex. It is formed of upright battens bolted to round wooden bars across the back, and bound with plain iron straps. The wooden structure of the door does not greatly alter in the succeeding age, the battens being fixed to oak cross beams or ledges; occasionally, as at Castle Hedingham (Essex) the battens have a joggled instead of an upright joint. It is, however, in the ironwork[2] of the twelfth-century doors that their chief interest is centred. In its simplest form this consists of a pair of strap-hinges which clasp the door both within and without, along the lines of the wooden ledges; on the butt of the door these straps are welded to the rings by which the door is hung on the staples bedded in the masonry of the door-jamb. These strap-hinges are commonly enriched with cross-hatching or some other form of simple ornament. At an early period they were strengthened by the addition of semicircular bands springing from the base of the hinge, and by other bands and pieces of metal all of which served to keep the battens in place as well as to enrich the appearance of the door. A fair number of doors, so ornamented, have survived in various parts of the country though seldom in a complete state. They can rarely be dated except on the assumption that they are contemporary with the doorway in which they hang. On this assumption the great majority belong to the middle or latter half of the twelfth century, though some few, of simpler form, may be earlier. At Eastwood (Essex), Haddiscoe (Norfolk), and elsewhere the straps are

---

[1] The glass at Lanchester (Durham), sometimes assigned to the twelfth century, was almost certainly made for the existing early thirteenth-century east window, *Proc. Soc. Ants.*, xxvii, p. 205.

[2] J. Starkie Gardner (revised by W. W. Watts), *Ironwork*, Pt. I, 1927; C. ffoulkes, *Decorative Ironwork*, 1913.

enriched by scrolled ornaments, and at Much Hormead (Herts.) the back of the door is panelled with ironwork in scrolled or geometrical designs. At Stillingfleet (Yorks.) and Staplehurst (Kent) the isolated pieces of ironwork (Pl. 40) take the form of strips, human or beast figures, crosses, &c. The most elaborate example of twelfth-century iron-work, however, is to be found on the west processional door from the cloister at Durham. The door is in two leaves and is completely covered with scrolled ironwork, in which the two pairs of hinges form the predominant parts of the design.

The church-doors of this age were perhaps generally secured by a stock-lock, but few of these have survived. The use of the draw-bar, common in inhabited buildings, cannot obviously have been used in all the doors of a church as it was operated from the inside.

One recorded instance of the use of bronze doors in England must be mentioned. At Bury St. Edmunds Abbey the great west doors, set up under Abbot Anselm (1121–48), were the work of Master Hugh, and it is related that 'as in his other works he surpassed every one else so in the making of these gates he surpassed himself'; they were 'arte fusoria', cast work, and perhaps resembled the contemporary bronze doors of several great churches of southern Italy.[1]

A few doors in England still retain the bronze knockers or handles, commonly called Sanctuary knockers. The best known example of these is the fine lion's head with a ring in its jaws on the north door at Durham. This is certainly of the twelfth century, as is the small head at Dormington (Hereford), but the others, such as that at St. Gregory, Norwich, are of later date.

In Winchester Cathedral are portions of a grate of scrolled ironwork which formerly enclosed the shrine of St. Swithun. It is commonly assigned to the close of the eleventh century, but differs little in character from work of a much later age.

---

[1] M. R. James in *Camb. Antiq. Soc. Comms.*, xxviii, p. 128.

PLATE 40

STAPLEHURST, KENT, S. DOOR
12th century

PLATE 41

DORCHESTER ABBEY, OXON., LEAD FONT
late 12th century

CASTLE FROME CHURCH, HEREFORDSHIRE, FONT
c. 1150

Piscinae and Stoups. The simplest form of piscina is formed by a shallow sinking or drain in the pavement or step near the altar. This was a common form in the larger monastic churches where a row of altars closely adjoined one another, and several examples have been found in recent excavations. The commonest form in the ordinary twelfth-century parish church would appear to have been the pillar-piscina, judging from the numerous fragments which have survived all over the country. The pillar-piscina consists of a small shaft set against the wall, with a base and capital, the top of the latter being sunk to form a drain. The drain set in a recess in the wall at the side, and to the south of the altar, also early makes its appearance. The recess may be of the simplest round-headed form, as at St. Martin's, Canterbury, or elaborately ornamented as in the example at St. Mary in Castro, Leicester.

Very few twelfth-century stoups have survived, nor do we know the common form of this fitting at that period. The example at Kilpeck is of cylindrical form curved in to a waist in the middle. It is clasped by a crude figure cut in low relief, and may date from *c.* 1150, about which time the church was built.

Fonts.[1] Fonts are undoubtedly the most commonly surviving fitting of eleventh- and twelfth century churches, and as many of them display considerable elaboration they have formed a favourite subject for monographs, both large and small. It is a curious fact that hardly any pre-Conquest example is above suspicion, and the great majority of supposed Saxon fonts were certainly not made for their present purpose.

Anglo-Norman fonts are divisible, by their form, into three main classes—cylindrical, square, and bowl-shaped, and also into certain local groups. Others again stand apart by reason of their material. The cylindrical and square fonts without stems are perhaps the earliest forms, the

[1] F. Bond, *Fonts and Font-covers*, 1908; E. T. Green, *Baptismal Fonts*, 1928.

cutting-down of the bowl, and the raising of it on a stem or group of shafts, being a later development. Both the square and cylindrical form afford an extensive field for decorative carving, and it is on these forms that the more elaborate compositions are to be found.

The cylindrical form, without a stem, is widely diffused. Elaborate examples with figures under a continuous arcade may be seen at Stoneleigh (apostles with their names), Wansford (Northants), Orleton (Hereford), and a late example at Stanton Fitzwarren (Wilts.). At Brighton and North Grimston (Yorks.) are representations of the Last Supper, and at St. Martin, Canterbury, is a twelfth-century font with geometrical ornament of interlaced circles; this font is also remarkable as built up of small stones. The shortened cylindrical bowl set on a stem may be seen at Kirkby (Lancs.) and Morville (Salop).

The square form is generally enriched with small shafts worked on the angles, and often has elaborate carving on each face. Mention may be made of that at West Haddon (Northants) with scenes from the life of Christ, Bridekirk (Cumberland) with beasts, foliage, &c., and the very curious font at Lenton (Notts.)[1] with figure-subjects of early and rather eastern character. The square font, when shortened, was commonly set on five supporting shafts, a larger central shaft, and four smaller ones at the angles. This was the common form in fonts of Purbeck or Tournai marble; in the former material they commonly have simple arcading on the faces, but the latter form a striking group which will be dealt with later.

The bowl-shaped type is that susceptible of the greatest number of variations. The hemispherical is the simplest form, and must necessarily be supported on a round stem or plinth. This form is represented by the fonts of the Herefordshire group, to be referred to later, and by a

---

[1] *Rel. and Ill. Arch.*, xv, p. 250. The carving has afinities with some German work of the twelfth century.

PLATE 42

SOUTHROP CHURCH, GLOS., FONT
late 12th century

SHERNBORNE CHURCH, NORFOLK, FONT
late 12th century

PLATE 43

AYLESBURY CHURCH, BUCKS., FONT
c. 1170–80

SHERBORNE ABBEY, TOMB OF ABBOT CLEMENT
c. 1160–5

number of examples of very varied character scattered over
the country. Those at Great Kimble (Bucks.) and Hay-
dock (Cornwall) have bases in the form of inverted scalloped capitals.

An elaboration of this form is produced by adding four
ears to the rim of the bowl, and supporting them by as
many additional shafts. This is the form of the so-called
Bodmin group in Cornwall. A second, late twelfth-century,
form is found in Herefordshire, where there are a series of
round bowls, of ovolo section, made of a local breccia. One
of these, at Kilpeck, is very large, and rests on five shafts.
A third form partakes of the outline of a cushion or a
scalloped capital, and may be seen at Upton (Hunts.) and
Springfield (Essex), the latter with rich foliage of late
character.

Local types of fonts have been recognized in Cornwall,
Herefordshire, West Norfolk, and Buckinghamshire. The
first of these[1] has been referred to above and centres round
Bodmin. The examples at that place, Key, St. Cuby, and
elsewhere are distinguished by much richness of foliage
ornament. The Herefordshire type is distinguished by great
elaboration of interlacing ornament and the queer figures
which can also be seen in the local architecture. There are
examples at Castle Frome (Pl. 41) and Eardisley and outside
the county, others with rather more restrained ornament
at Shottesdon (Salop) and Chaddesley Corbet (Worcs.).
The West Norfolk group is distinguished by having square
bowls set on angle-shafts. The fonts at Toftrees, with
simple interlacing designs, at Shernborne (Pl. 42) and at
Scunthorpe with the Adoration of the Magi are the more
important examples. The Aylesbury group is marked by
its fluted hemispherical bowl as at Aylesbury (Pl. 43), Bled-
low, and elsewhere.

Fonts made of Tournai marble or touch are widely
scattered, but infrequent; to the examples collected by

[1] E. H. Sedding, *Norman Architecture in Cornwall*, 1909.

Mr. C. J. Eden[1] may be added a mutilated bowl in the Museum at Ipswich. All are of the same type, a square bowl set on five shafts, and bear a close resemblance to examples in the same material on the continent. The faces of all the examples are carved, either with conventional designs or with figure-subjects, as at Winchester (Legend of St. Nicholas) or East Meon, Hants (Adam and Eve).

Leaden fonts[2] (Pl. 41) form a class by themselves; of the thirty-one which are known to survive, some fifteen or sixteen may be ascribed to the twelfth century. Of these the six in Gloucestershire are all cast from the same pattern. The fonts are all, except one, of cylindrical form, and the great majority have a continuous arcade with figures below; at Ashover there are twenty-seven figures. At Brookland (Kent) there is a double range of arches with the signs of the Zodiac above and the works of the months below. Scrolled foliage is the staple motive at Barnetby-le-Wold (Lincs.), and Edburton (Sussex).

Monuments. Funeral monuments assignable to the late eleventh and the twelfth century are extremely infrequent in England. Contemporary and later chroniclers often record epitaphs on tombs of this age, but in only a few instances have any remains of these survived. Commonly, no doubt, they were painted either on the tomb or on boards hanging beside it, and have consequently perished. In more than one of the surviving cut inscriptions there is an exasperating absence of the name of the deceased, and in consequence a date can only be assigned from the character of the ornament.

Monumental effigies first make their appearance in England in the twelfth century,[3] the earliest example being

---

[1] Winchester Cath., East Meon, St. Mary, Bourne, and St. Michael, Southampton, Lincoln Cath., Thornton Curtis (Lincs.), and St. Peter, Ipswich. C. J. Eden, *Black Tournai Fonts in England* (1909).

[2] A. C. Fryer, 'Notes on leaden Fonts', *Arch. Journ.*, lvii, p. 40; Additional notes, *ibid.*, lxxviii, p. 296; L. Weaver in *Archit. Rev.*, xix, p. 99.

[3] Above the north transept doorway at Norwich is a figure of a bishop (Pl. 30)

the much worn figure of an abbot at Westminster, assigned
with every probability to Gilbert Crispin, 1121. This
early form is cut in low relief in a sunk panel, so that the
general surface is flat. Superiors of religious houses in the
twelfth century were commonly buried under the floor of
the chapter-house, where a raised slab was an encum-
brance. All the other surviving early effigies would
appear to belong to the middle or second half of the century, and most of them, in consequence, show a marked
advance on the simple figure at Westminster. Two tombs
(Pl. 44) of bishops at Salisbury[1] were undoubtedly moved
there from Old Sarum about 1227. One of these is flat, and
has the figure of the bishop under a shallow trefoiled arch
with rich banded acanthus ornament round the sides; the
other is simpler, and has a long laudatory inscription without
mentioning the name; certain particulars, however, make it
applicable to Bishop Jocelyn, 1184. At Peterborough[2] are
two effigies (Pl. 44) of abbots in high relief with architectural
canopies over their heads; both were brought from the
chapter-house and may be assigned to the second half of the
century. Ely[3] contains a slab (Pl. 45) of the same character
(found at St. Mary's church); under the canopy is a large
figure of St. Michael with the soul of the deceased, who was
presumably a bishop as he has a crozier. At Sherborne
Abbey[4] is the upper part of another effigy (Pl. 43) with an inscription commemorating Abbot Clement (died c. 1160–5).
At Exeter[5] is an effigy ascribed to Bishop Bartholomew, 1184,
but the incipient sprouting on the scroll of the crozier, and
the advanced character of the capitals of the side-shafts, seem

---

under a round arch with side shafts. It is apparently in situ, and must date
from the early years of the twelfth century. The rendering of the figure is similar
to that of a monumental effigy, and it has a prime importance as perhaps the
earliest Anglo-Norman figure of this type now surviving.

[1] Stothard, *Monumental Effigies*. Prior and Gardner, *English Med. Fig. Sculpture*,
p. 573.
[2] Prior and Gardner, *op. cit.*, p. 575.
[3] Ibid., *op. cit.*, p. 84.   [4] *Arch. Journ.*, xiii, p. 288.
[5] J. Britton, *Exeter Cathedral* (1836), Pl. XX.

to demand a date of *c.* 1200. There is also a slab with a figure of an abbot at Abbotsbury of about the same age.

All these are cut on tapering slabs, and undoubtedly formed the actual lids of coffins.

Coffin-lids of a simpler type can be met with in some variety. The form most cognate to the effigy is that which became common in the thirteenth century as a memorial to the head of a monastic house. It bears an upright crozier grasped by a hand which issues from the side of the slab. The earliest example in England is probably that found at Welbeck[1] (founded *c.* 1153) and no doubt commemorating one of the earliest abbots. Here the crozier is of the uncommon tau-form. Another example, which may belong to the close of the twelfth century, is at Romsey Abbey.[2] Perhaps of the same age is a slab in Newcastle Castle chapel[3] with plain sword and an inscription in early capitals. Slabs with crosses of the simplest form, no doubt, also date from the twelfth century; a good example has been found at Lincoln.[4] A remarkable slab of Tournai marble, found in the chapterhouse at Lewes Priory[5] and now in St. John's, Southover, has a long inscription commemorating Gundrada (died 1085), wife of the founder, William de Warenne; it is, so far, unparalleled in England, and, if native work, can hardly be earlier than the middle of the twelfth century. It bears a double row of rich, banded acanthus ornament not unlike that on the slab at Salisbury.

At Bridlington Priory (Yorks.) is one with a curious sectional representation of a church, flying dragons above, and beasts below,[6] and at Bishopstone (Sussex) is a second with a pair of peacocks and the Agnus Dei. The former is no doubt of the twelfth century, but the latter is of doubtful date.

[1] Gough, *Sepulchral Mons.*, i, Plates, p. cviii.
[2] C. Boutell, *Christ. Mons.*, p. 54.
[3] C. Burtell, *op. cit.*, p. 84.   [4] Gough, *op. cit.*, i, Pl. LIII.
[5] W. H. Godfrey, *The Church of St. John Bap. Southover*, 1927.
[6] W. Richardson, *Mon. Ruins of Yorks.*, ii, pp. 62–3.

PLATE 44

PETERBOROUGH CATHEDRAL, EFFIGY OF ABBOT
late 12th century

SALISBURY CATHEDRAL, EFFIGY OF BISHOP
late 12th century

PLATE 45

ELY CATHEDRAL, TOMB SLAB
late 12th century

OLD SARUM, TOMBS IN CEMETERY
late 12th century

Yet another variant is the slab at Lincoln (assigned to St. Remigius but of much later date) which is carved with a Jesse tree.

Another type of coffin-lid is the coped or ridged slab. The best-known example is that at Winchester, long ascribed to William Rufus, but probably covering the remains of Bishop Henry of Blois (died 1171, to which period seem to belong the contents[1] of the tomb). This lid is of marble and of simple coped form with moulded edges. Two ridged coffin-lids, one covered with shallow cheveron ornament and the other with an indication of roof-tiles,[2] have survived at Bakewell (Derby). Others have been found in the cemetery at Old Sarum.

When these flat or ridged slabs covered a burial in the open air they were often provided with head- and foot-stones (Pl. 45). A most important collection of these was found during the excavations at Old Sarum in 1912–13.[3] The upright stones were commonly carved with a cross or some other ornament; two of the flat slabs bore a wheel-head cross standing on a stepped Calvary, and two had inscriptions. One inscription was to a certain Alward of Ramsbury, who may perhaps be dated in the first half of the twelfth century, but all these memorials must have been set up before the removal of the cathedral-body to Salisbury in 1227.

Head-stones of the same type as those at Sarum are to be met with occasionally in various parts of the country; there are a number at Bakewell[4] (Derby) and others at Whitby Abbey and Lyminge (Kent).

Two other forms of memorials must be mentioned both of an uncommon type. The first is the free-standing wheel-head cross, with a carved stem, exemplified at Fletton[5] (Hunts.) and Kelloe (Durham). It is in the direct Saxon

[1] *Arch.*, xiii, p. 309.   [2] Boutell, *op. cit.*, p. 13.
[3] *Proc. Soc. Ants.*, xxvi, p. 107–17.   [4] *Arch. Journ.*, iv, p. 57.
[5] *Roy. Com. on Hist. Mons., Hunts.*, Pl. 50.

tradition, the first bears an inscription to William Fitzralph and the ornament on both is not earlier than the twelfth century. The second form is that of a solid stone ark with a ridged and gabled top to be seen at Fordwich[1] (Kent). The sides are arcaded and the top has scale ornament to represent tiles.

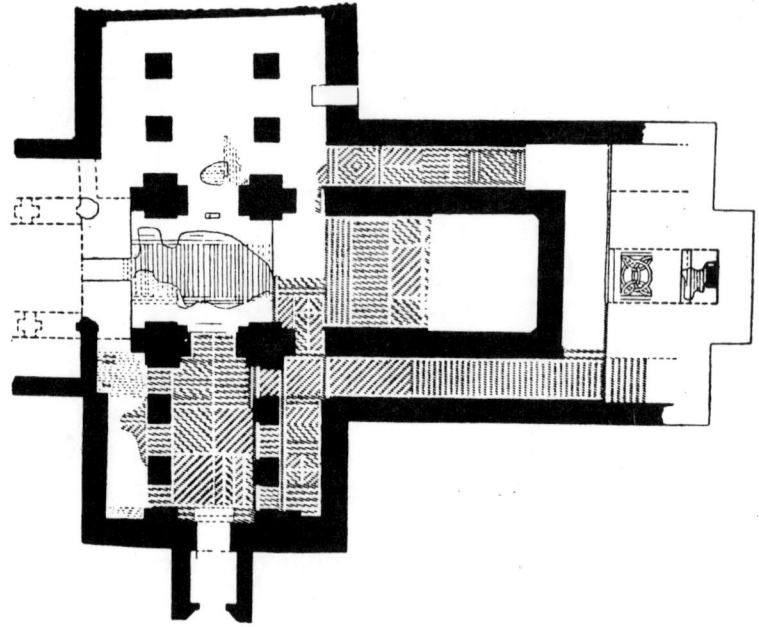

FIG. 43. Old Sarum Cathedral. Pavement.

It was a not infrequent practice to place within the actual grave a leaden plate or cross[2] inscribed with the name of the deceased. Such are the plates found in the late twelfth-century tombs of the Saxon kings of Kent[3] at St. Augustine's, Canterbury, and the cross, reputed to have been found in the grave of King Arthur[4] at Glastonbury. A lead plate of this nature was found in 1670 in

[1] *Arch. Journ.*, lxxxvi, p. 259.
[2] Lead crosses with inscriptions, probably of the period immediately before the Conquest, have been found at Lincoln (*Proc. Arch. Instit.*, 1848, Lincoln, p. xliv) and at St. Augustine's, Canterbury, dated 1063 (*Antiq. Journ.*, iv, p. 422).
[3] *Arch. Cant.*, xxxviii, p. 97.   [4] Camden, *Britannia* (edit. 1607), p. 166.

PLATE 46

KEMPLEY CHURCH, GLOS., PAINTING
OF APOSTLES
late 12th century

PETERBOROUGH CATHEDRAL, NAVE CEILING
c. 1180–90

PLATE 47

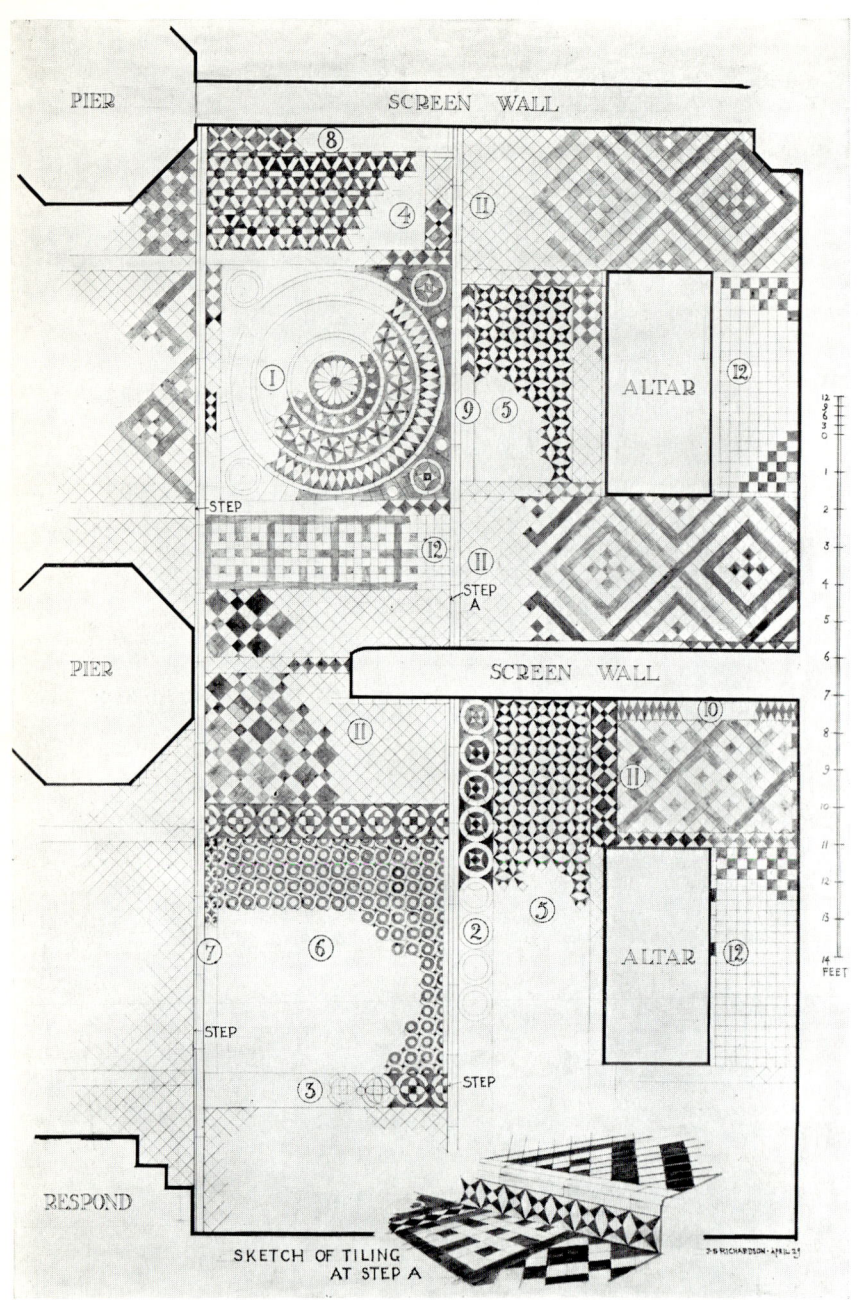

BYLAND ABBEY, PAVEMENT IN S. TRANSEPT CHAPELS
c. 1180–90

Lincoln Cathedral;[1] it dates from the reign of William Rufus. It is remarkable as containing a reference to Bishop Remi 'who built this church', which seems hardly appropriate to a plate intended to be buried in a grave. Others commemorating Archbishop Theobald, 1161, and Prior Almer, 1137, have been found in Canterbury Cathedral.[2]

Paving. It is not often that any remains of the original paving of an Anglo-Norman church has survived, and it is only by the occasional discovery of early pavement covered by those of later date that any evidence can be obtained of its nature. It seems probable, from information so obtained, that the general covering of the floor of an Anglo-Norman church was of stone slabs of small dimensions or, after the middle of the twelfth century,[3] of plain square red tiles.

The excavations at Old Sarum showed that Bishop Roger's early twelfth-century church was paved (Fig. 43) with alternate squares of white Chilmark and green Hurdcote stone.[4]

Towards the close of the twelfth century this simple covering gave place to a more elaborate system, at any rate for the altar-platforms and more important parts of the building. The recent excavations at Byland Abbey (Yorks.) have uncovered considerable stretches (Pl. 47) of such pavement,[5] fortunately preserved largely intact. They may be considered to date from the completion of the eastern part of the church (*c.* 1180–90) and consist of shaped tiles, of two contrasting tints, set in an elaborate mosaic of circles and diaper pattern. Tiles of a similar type have been found on the site of Meaux Abbey[6] (Yorks.), and at Rievaulx Abbey (Yorks.).

---

[1] *Proc. Arch. Instit.*, 1848, Lincoln, p. 248.   [2] *Arch.*, xv, p. 295.

[3] The earliest use of brick in England, apart from the re-use of ancient material, is also to be placed, probably, in the latter part of the twelfth century. To this date belong the shaped bricks used in the Infirmary of Coggeshall Abbey (Essex) and no doubt made locally.   [4] *Proc. Soc. Ants.*, xxvi, p. 107.

[5] *Proc. Soc. Ants. Scotland*, 6th ser., iii, p. 288. Similar but rather later pavements have been found at Newbattle and Melrose Abbeys. *Ibid.*

[6] *E. Riding Antiq. Soc. Trans.*, xxvi, p. 106.

INDEX

Aachen, Charlemagne's Palace-chapel, 112.

Abaci, **100, 121–2.**

Abbotsbury, effigy of abbot, 158.

Adam and Eve, represented on font, 156; painted representation of,147.

Adel, beak-head ornament, 131 n.; carved orders, 132; doorway, 108.

Adoration of the Magi, represented on font, 155; on tympanum, 137; painting of, 147.

Agnus Dei, represented on coffin-lid, 158; on tympana, 137.

Albert, Abp. of York, 118.

Alexander, Bp., building at Lincoln by, 22, 144.

Almer, Prior, lead plate commemorating, 161.

Alne, ornament, 132.

Alternating supports, *see* Double-bays.

Alward of Ramsbury, monument to, 159.

Amberley (Sussex), capitals, 135 n.

Amwell, Great, plan, 104; windows, 68 n.

Ancaster stone, 113.

Anglo-Saxon Chronicle, cited, 45.

Anselm, Abt., bronze doors at Bury St. Edmunds set up by, 152; nave completed by, 30.

Apocalypse, The Elders of The, painting of, 147.

Apostles, representations of, Copford, 146; Kempley, 147; Malmesbury, 144; Stoneleigh, 154.

Apses, in Parish Churches, 101; *see also under* Plans.

Araines, vaulting, 98 n.

Arcading, 108, **133**; Bishop's Cleeve, 133; Bolton, 133; Castle Rising, 108; Christchurch, 133; Devizes, 108, 133; Durham, 133; Norwich, 133.

Arches, cusped, 132 n.; diaphragm, 5–8.

Arch-mouldings, 9, **122.**

Arthur, King, lead cross reputed to have been found in grave of, 160.

Ashlar masonry, 116.

Ashleworth, herring-bone masonry, 115.

Ashover, lead font, 156.

Askham Bryan, plan, 102.

Aslakeby (Templar), plan, 110.

Aston Eyre, tympanum, 137, 141.

Augustinian or Austin Canons, development of Order of, 70, 83–4; buildings in England, 83–4.

Aylesbury, font, 155.

Bakewell, coffin-lids, 159; headstones, 159.

Baldwin, Abt., Bury St. Edmunds begun by, 30.

Bampton, herring-bone masonry, 115.

Bapchild, destroyed plan, 105,

Barfreston, carved orders, 133; ornament, 108 (Greek key), 129; painted decoration, 146, 147; tympanum, 137; windows, 68.

Barking Abbey (Benedictine nuns), plan, 43.

Barnack, carved 'Majesty', 141 n.

Barnack stone, 113, 114; used at Rochester, 66.

Barnetby-le-Wold, lead font, 156.

Barrington, Little, tympanum, 141.

Bartholomew, Bp. of Exeter, effigy ascribed to, 157.

Barton St. Mary, beak-head ornament, 131 n.

Base-mouldings, **119–21**; in Normandy, 16.

Bases, **136**; shafts set on backs of animals, Colchester, 136 n.; Sutton (Northants), 136 n.; spur ornaments, Bath, 136; Hereford, 136; York, 136.

Bath Abbey (Benedictine), base-mouldings 119, 120; spur ornaments, 136; west front, 63; see transferred from Wells, 18.

Bath stone, 113.

Battle Abbey (Benedictine), **28,** 37; colonized from Marmoutier, 16, 28; excavations, 29; plan, 16, 28–9.

Bayeux:
Cathedral, base-mouldings, 17 n.; beak-head ornament, 131; carved capitals in crypt, 16 n.; crypt, 12, 64; transept gallery, 13.
S. Vigor Priory, diaphragm-arches, 6; plan, 13 n.

PRINTED IN GREAT BRITAIN AT THE UNIVERSITY PRESS, OXFORD
BY VIVIAN RIDLER, PRINTER TO THE UNIVERSITY